The Elastic Closet

# The Elastic Closet

## A History of Homosexuality in France, 1942–present

Scott Gunther
*Assistant Professor of French, Wellesley College, USA*

palgrave
macmillan

First published 2009 by
PALGRAVE MACMILLAN

Palgrave Macmillan in the UK is an imprint of Macmillan Publishers Limited, registered in England, company number 785998, of Houndmills, Basingstoke, Hampshire RG21 6XS.

Palgrave Macmillan in the US is a division of St Martin's Press LLC, 175 Fifth Avenue, New York, NY 10010.

Palgrave Macmillan is the global academic imprint of the above companies and has companies and representatives throughout the world.

Palgrave® and Macmillan® are registered trademarks in the United States, the United Kingdom, Europe and other countries.

ISBN-13: 978–0–230–22105–5 hardback
ISBN-10: 0–230–22105–X hardback

This book is printed on paper suitable for recycling and made from fully managed and sustained forest sources. Logging, pulping and manufacturing processes are expected to conform to the environmental regulations of the country of origin.

A catalogue record for this book is available from the British Library.

Library of Congress Cataloging-in-Publication Data

Gunther, Scott Eric.
    The elastic closet : a history of homosexuality in France, 1942–present / Scott Gunther.
        p. cm.
    Includes bibliographical references and index.
    ISBN 978–0–230–22105–5 (alk. paper)
        1. Homosexuality – France – History – 20th century. I. Title.

HQ76.3.F8G86 2009
306.76'6094409045—dc22                                    2008029963

10   9   8   7   6   5   4   3   2   1
18  17  16  15  14  13  12  11  10  09

Printed and bound in Great Britain by
CPI Antony Rowe, Chippenham and Eastbourne

# Contents

# Illustrations

## Tables

## Figures

# Acknowledgements

I am happy to have this chance to thank Herrick Chapman, Bryant T. (Tip) Ragan, Eric Fassin, Marie-Elisabeth Handman, and Shanny Peer for generously spending countless hours reading drafts, offering perceptive suggestions and criticisms, and encouraging me throughout this project. I also want to thank Michael Strang and Ruth Ireland at Palgrave who have given such careful attention and direction to this project. I am indebted to French Cultural Services for the Chateaubriand grant, which allowed me to conduct preliminary research for this project in France. I am especially thankful for the guidance and encouragement of my colleagues in the Wellesley French Department and for the generous support of Wellesley College during the 2006–2007 academic year, which allowed me to conduct new research and to prepare the manuscript for publication. I would like to recognize the assistance offered by individuals at *Gai pied* in Paris, the *Archives de la Préfecture de Police de Paris*, the *Archives du Sénat,* and the television station PinkTV, who made their archival materials available to me and facilitated access to essential sources. I thank Jan-Paul Pouliquen, Gérard Bach-Ignasse, Jean-Pierre Michel, and members of the *Gais retraités* for graciously agreeing to be interviewed. I am also grateful to Marc Boninchi, Gérard Bach-Ignasse, Jan-Paul Pouliquen, and Jean-Pierre Michel for making documents from their own research available to me.

My greatest debt is undoubtedly to friends, Sealing Cheng, Julie Fette, Pam Gillons, Stacie Goddard, Arne Grafweg, Jean-Christophe Groffe, Yvon Guy, Yong Kim, Paul MacDonald, Molly McCarthy, Alex Morel, Fabrice Morel, Alejandra Osorio, Lauren Pickard, William Poulin-Deltour, Jennie Pyers, Nikhil Rao, Andy Shapiro, Aline Silhouette, Stacy Sneeringer, Sylvie Waskiewicz, Astrid Weinstock, Jeffrey Weinstock, and Molly White, the Avila and Molina families, to my sisters, Kammi and Danielle, and to my parents, Judy and Dennis, who have been there for me in the most important ways since the project's beginning. I offer special thanks to Rick Siggins for the enthusiasm he has brought over the years to hashing out the book's ideas; to my sister, Laura Gunther, for designing a cover by which I would feel proud to have anyone judge the book; and to Guillermo Avila, whose intellectual freshness and lucidity continue to push me in new and frequently unexpected directions.

# Introduction: Republican Values and the Depenalization of Sodomy in France

> "I am first human, then citizen and finally homosexual."
> What a lovely hierarchy! We were really naïve to imagine
> that by hiding behind concepts of ordinary heterosexual
> normality, we could attain any integration whatsoever. It
> was self-mutilation pure and simple. With wounds that will
> never heal.[1]
>
> Joseph-Marie Hulewicz, former editor of *Gai pied hebdo*[2]

Like any good closet, the French Republic has served both to protect
and to restrain. French people who engage in same-sex sexual practices have largely escaped the kind of legal repression seen in other
countries over the last two hundred years – in fact, France was
the first country in Europe to legalize sodomy as early as 1791. Yet
despite this legal tolerance, French homosexuals have been inclined
to live their sexuality more discretely and to embrace identity politics
with less enthusiasm than their American counterparts. Indeed, the
values of the Republic have managed to keep expressions of both pro-
homosexual and antihomosexual sentiments within a narrower range
in France than has been the case in places like the United States – a
country where both "gay pride" and homophobia have tended to be
expressed more aggressively.

The French Republic has protected its homosexual citizens primarily through the core values of *secularism, separation between public and
private spheres, liberalism,* and *universalism*; together these values have
been responsible for keeping homosexuality legal in France and for
limiting the possibilities for the most overt forms of homophobia.
Following the Revolution of 1789, respect for *secularist principles* led to

the elimination of all "crimes of superstition," which included things such as witchcraft and blasphemy, but would have also included sodomy (defined here as homosexual acts between consenting adults), since it originated in Christianity and many philosophers had begun to argue that there was no rational basis for punishing it. In addition, the strong separation between public and private spheres in republican France has meant that the criminalization of consensual acts in private would be widely perceived as an unjustifiable invasion of privacy. Even more importantly, given that it is hard to imagine who the victim of sexual activity between consenting adults might be, the crime of sodomy would have violated the basic principle of classical *liberalism* that every crime must have an ascertainable victim.

Of course, many countries have shared the basic notion that laws should avoid punishing people for victimless crimes; so why was it easier for other liberal democracies to maintain sodomy as a crime than it was for France? The answer once again has to do with the particularities of French republicanism. In this case, the *universalist* vision of French law requires that basic legal principles be applied consistently, without any exceptions. While other legal systems can occasionally accommodate exceptions to their basic legal principles – particularly, when like in the case of sodomy, there is a long tradition of doing so – the universalist aspirations of the French republican legal system make this especially difficult. The rigidity of the French republican legal system in this respect has protected French people who engage in same-sex sexual acts from various forms of legal repression; because though French lawmakers may have wanted to reinstate the crime of sodomy at various moments since 1791, they have not had the license to do so.

But French republicanism has also created restraints. The strong separation between public and private spheres means that the American notion that "the personal is political" has resonated differently in the context of France, and public displays of sexual identity have not always been well received. Since the universalist discourse of French republicanism maintains that the opportunity to be socially integrated exists in principle for anyone willing to accept the restrictions of assimilation, tolerance of difference is not what is called for.

In recent decades, the French rhetoric of universalism has stymied French homosexuals from mobilizing politically around sexual identities and has encouraged various manifestations of social respectability along with a surprisingly strong reverence for heter-onormative values. Beginning in the early 1980s in particular, French gays and lesbians began to portray themselves in increasingly socially acceptable ways, as hardworking and decent folks who formed stable relationships and who presented little threat to the status quo. New movements and journals appeared in the early 80s that made every effort to distance themselves from the less palatable aspects of earl-ier movements – particularly the pedophilic, sadomasochistic, trans-sexual, transvestite, promiscuous, and public-sex elements. This change in self-representations by French gays and lesbians raises the question of whether it was public opinion of homosexuality or the meaning of what it is to be homosexual that underwent greater change in those years. There is reason to doubt that social attitudes changed radically in France in the 1980s, to the extent that gays' self-representations merely came more into alignment with the Republic's longstanding requirements for assimilation and acceptance.

What is presented here is a history of French homosexuals from Second World War to the present in the interconnected realms of law (from a discriminatory law enacted in 1942 under Vichy regarding sexual majority to anti-hate speech legislation in 2004), politics (from the homophile movements of the 1950s to a distinctly French articu-lation of queer radicalism in recent years), and the media (from the journal *Arcadie* in the 1950s to *Têtu* and PinkTV today) with a focus on the complex relationship between French republican values and the possibilities they have offered for change in each of these spheres. This focus relies on several interrelated arguments: first, that changes in the legal treatment of French homosexuals can occur independently of parallel shifts in widespread attitudes toward homosexuality, which are often best explained in terms of their continuity; second, that the recent history of homosexuality in France cannot be understood as a simple teleological progression toward ever greater freedom for homo-sexuals beginning in the mid-twentieth century and continuing up to the present, but as a complicated series of strategies adapted to each time period that have at times actually served to limit the freedoms of French homosexuals; and finally, that challenges to republican values have not been terribly effective – the resiliency and elasticity of repub-lican discourse have made it difficult to subvert.

Though the book's title uses the gender-neutral term homo-sexuality, readers will notice that lesbians are less present in the first chapters than at the end. The first part of the book looks at what legislators, judges, and medical doctors had to say about homosexuality. The fact is that while nineteenth-century and early-twentieth-century writers and artists were interested in representing lesbians in their works, medical "experts," lawmakers and judges were paying less attention to their existence – for better or for worse.[3] Even the sections of the book examining later periods reflect the fact that as late as the 1970s and 80s, French gay movements were almost exclusively male and for the most part, openly misogynist. Lesbian militants tended to find one another in women's liberation movements, such as the *Mouvement de libération des femmes* (or its satellite organization the *Gouines rouges*), as opposed to trying to fight for attention in gay groups that claimed to serve both men and women. The French press has not been much better. Media sources that have declared themselves to be for both gay men and women, such as the magazine *Têtu*, offer almost nothing for lesbians. And while there are now two magazines explicitly designed for lesbians, *Lesbia* and *La Dixième Muse*, neither has managed to attract large numbers of readers. Given the lack of space offered to lesbians by the mainstream gay political movements and media sources, it is hardly surprising that an overwhelming majority of those involved in the nascent radical queer movement in France are women.

This book is divided into four chapters ordered chronologically along with an introduction that provides background information on the repeal of the crime of sodomy in France in 1791, a summary of the mechanisms of the French republican legal system that have forced lawmakers to keep homosexuality legal ever since, and a quick look at the ways in which nineteenth-century police, judges and medical legal "experts" looked for ways to control homosexuality in the absence of discriminatory laws. After this historical overview, the first chapter ("It Could Have Been Worse") begins by looking at the period from 1942 to 1968, a time when French legislators, unable to reinstate the crime of sodomy, adapted their strategies and contented themselves with two juridically acceptable, but somewhat inconsequential laws that satisfied French law's requirement that every crime have a victim. The first law, enacted in 1942 under the Vichy government, found victims in France's youth and expanded this class of potential victims by raising the age of sexual majority for homosexuals to 21.[4] The second, passed in 1960, found its victim in the public and doubled the penalty for public indecency when it involved people of the same sex. The story of both of these laws serves as an example of how the liberal values and the universalist spirit of the Republic's legal system protected gay people from more extreme forms of legal repression.

The second chapter ("Attempts at Subversion") examines the period of the 1970s, a time when the discriminatory laws from the previous period remained in force while the most radical forms of political action ever witnessed appeared. This exceptional period in the history of gay political strategies offers an example of the resiliency and elasticity of republican values and their capacity to withstand attempts to subvert. The analysis of the political radicalism of the early 70s raises the question as to what forms of political action are most effective in producing legal change in the context of France. Can a stringently anti-assimilationist, anti-republican political stance be effective? If the laboratory of the early 70s tells us anything, the answer is no. Political groups' radical demands proved entirely incapable of producing legal change, and it was only after more assimilationist movements appeared in the late 70s that real legal change occurred.

Legal, political, and cultural changes since the 1980s are the subject of the third chapter ("French Homosexuals Build a More Stately Closet"). Between 1980 and 1982, the two discriminatory laws from 1942 and 1960 were repealed and French gays and lesbians were offered new opportunities for social normalization and assimilation. In the 1980s, French homosexuals began to create a new space for themselves, a space that in many ways was better than the one they had just come out of. Certainly, the new face of homosexuality led to a number of positive changes: opportunities for social assimilation increased and gay political groups successfully lobbied for an antidiscrimination law in 1985, for legally recognized partnerships for same-sex couples in 1999 (the *pacte civil de solidarité* or "PaCS") and for an anti-hate-speech law in 2004. However, it is also possible to see the ways in which deference to the French republican model of assimilation during this time reproduced some form of "closet." Beginning in the 1980s, control was no longer exerted downward through legal restrictions, but inward. After years of legal censure, French gay people had learned that external control was possible, that it would remain a threat, and that to escape future censure and to preserve society's new degree of tolerance, they had to replace external controls with self-control.

Finally, the fourth chapter ("'Outing' the French Gay Media") reflects on the influence of Republican universalist rhetoric on gay media from the 1990s up through the first decade of the twenty-first century. This final chapter turns to three contemporary media sources, the magazine *Têtu*, the magazine *Préférences*, and the French television station PinkTV, for its analysis of the ways in which interiorized forms of self-control continue to influence French gays' self-representations and prevent them from asserting difference even in their own media. For all three media sources studied here, it is clear that the target population is gay men, yet out of deference to French universalism, they have all felt the need to claim to be serving other, broader audiences. The goal here is to expose these media sources' true identities; to "out" them. The fact that these media sources cannot simply come out as entertainment for gay men on their own is an indication that French republicanism is alive and well today, and that over time the rhetoric of universalism has proved to be elastic enough to remain seductive.

## Republican values and the depenalization of sodomy

With the ratification of the Penal Code of 1791, France became the first country in the modern world to decriminalize sodomy.[5] On its face, this anomaly of French legal history might be taken to indicate that nineteenth-century France was a relatively tolerant space for people who practiced homosexual acts. Such a shallow analysis of legal change is, however, misleading: widespread social attitudes cannot be ascertained simply on the basis of the absence or presence of particular laws. Although the legal basis for criminalizing sodomy disappeared in 1791, various forms of repression continued over the course of the nineteenth century and into the twentieth century, and in some respects became more severe. Like other legal changes associated with the Revolution of 1789, the strong rupture in the legal treatment of sodomites was not reflected in social attitudes, which are best described in terms of their continuity.

Clearly, there are many reasons why a society's laws do not represent a mere codification of its citizens' general will. In a representative democracy, the actions of lawmakers are limited not only by constitutional constraints but also by political necessities. Even the desire for a constitutionally and politically viable form of state control may never make its way into legislation, particularly when other means of accomplishing the same goals exist. Indeed, with regard to homosexuality in nineteenth-century France, discriminatory laws proved somewhat unnecessary, to the degree that police, judges, and medicolegal "experts" of the time were able to exercise effective control through discriminatory uses and interpretations of existing, nondiscriminatory laws. Nevertheless, the French Revolution did represent an improvement for French sodomites as revolutionary ideals encouraged a remaking of French government and society – and even if social attitudes were slow to change, there is no doubt that things could have been worse, especially when one considers the legal penalties for sodomy in other countries at the time.

The absence of sodomy laws in France since 1791 represents a strong rupture not just across space but also across time. Viewed historically, the 1791 legal reform represents an exceptionally radical and abrupt break with the longstanding legal precedent for the crime of sodomy. Yet even given the surprising nature of this kind of abrupt legal change; an equally radical rupture in social attitudes would generally be more difficult to account for. Indeed, the implausible conclusion that French people after 1791 differed significantly from other Europeans of the same time or from French people prior to 1791 in their attitudes toward homosexuality seems to rely on a common but faulty assumption that a causal connection necessarily exists between legal and social change.

Before turning to a more detailed discussion of the relationship between the repeal of sodomy in 1791 and the continuity of widespread social attitudes toward homosexuality afterwards, it is useful at this point to look first at the forms of legal repression existing prior to 1791, beginning with original source of modern European legal systems: the Roman Empire.

Laws regulating homosexuality in modern Western societies generally, and in France in particular, have their origins in the legal system of Rome. Until the arrival of Constantine II, homosexuality was tolerated, provided that: (1) it did not interfere with the citizens' duties to the city; (2) the Roman citizen made use only of inferior persons, such as slaves, as pleasure objects; and (3) during the homosexual activity, the Roman citizen maintained the dominant or active role.[6] The first Roman law aiming to restrict homosexual acts in a more comprehensive way was not promulgated until 342, under Constantine II. It stated that "when a man behaves in bed in the way of a woman...the crime is one of which it is better not to speak...Consequently, we order that the law rise up, a sword in its hand, and strike the abominable man who has made himself guilty of such a crime, that this man be subject to an atrocious and refined chastisement."[7] Here the meaning of the punishment, "atrocious and refined chastisement," is not clear. Yet, in the centuries to come, the punishment associated with this crime "of which it is better not to speak" would become increasingly precisely defined in European legal systems.

During the Middle Ages, the conciliar and synodal rules of the Christian Church began to play a more central role in the repression of homosexuality. The most clear and damaging of these proclamations came from the Council of Nablus, which in 1120 had put together the most complete and coherent collection of canonical law, and the most severe with regard to "sins of the flesh" ever witnessed in the history of the Catholic Church. With these proclamations, homosexuality became punishable in no ambiguous terms by death through burning on the stake.[8] However, it was not until 1317 that the death penalty first enounced by the Council of Nablus claimed its first victim in France: a certain Robert de Péronne burned alive at the stake in Laon.[9] The number of documented cases of individuals condemned for sodomy[10] in France did not accelerate at this point, but rather remained fairly low in the years following. In fact, documentary evidence indicates that between 1317 and 1789, the number of individuals burned at the stake in France reached only thirty-eight. This is a relatively small number, especially when compared to the number of witches and charlatans executed during the same period.[11] Of the thirty-eight executed for sodomy, approximately one-third were accused of additional crimes including rapes and murders. It is extremely difficult to provide precise numbers, since there are immense voids in the archival records for executions of sodomites. These voids are primarily the result of the fact that when a sodomite[12] was burned at the stake, the documents associated with the trial were frequently burned along with him.[13]

Generally, it was the procedure of the French medieval legal system to eliminate all traces of the condemned individual's existence, including personal belongings and other property of the condemned, by throwing all these things together in the fire with him. It was also standard procedure, though no one can say with what frequency it was carried out, to destroy all documents associated with the condemned individual's trial at the time of his burning. The rationale for all of this was that this crime was of such a heinous character as to merit annihilating any evidence of the condemned individual's life. It can also be seen as evidence of a fear of contagion for other members of society through exposure to these objects or documents. Perhaps, it was thought that mere knowledge of the possibility of such a crime, which might come through reading the trial's documents, could inspire others to commit it.

In France, sodomy remained punishable by death until the early eighteenth century, when authorities began to rethink their motivations and strategies for controlling homosexuality. During the Renaissance and the Reformation, homosexuality had been conceived of and punished as a sin, as an abomination before God. The Enlightenment ideals of the early eighteenth century, however, encouraged a more rational and secular approach to punishment. Beginning in the 1720s, French judges and police relied on a new understanding of homosexuality as a disorder, as a socially unacceptable taste or leaning, which needed to be controlled, particularly because of its suspected connection with the criminal underworld.[14] With this shift in the understanding of the dangers of homosexuality, from sin to disorder, the executions of sodomites ceased. The new understanding of homosexuality required new forms of control and in the decades following, homosexuals became subject to greater surveillance. Police began to monitor homosexuals closely, to take note of their meeting places, and generally, to collect as much information about their behaviors as possible.

The shift in the early eighteenth century from sodomy as a sin against God to sodomy as a corrupting force of society is indicative of the growing influence of Enlightenment ideas, which called on human beings to take control of their own destinies. By the mid-eighteenth century, punishment in the form of public execution was no longer acceptable in France: the rationalization of punishment during this time corresponded with the notion that punishment for punishment's sake or on the grounds of revenge could no longer be justified. The only legitimate grounds for punishment were incapacitation (to prevent criminal recidivism) and deterrence. This rationalization of ideas of punishment corresponded with a shift in tangible forms of punishment, from burning at the stake to efforts to control, police, and monitor homosexual activities.

Some *philosophes*, including Condorcet, Montesquieu and Anacharsis Cloots, had expressed tolerant views of homosexuality, and even those like Voltaire, who felt contempt for homosexual practices, nonetheless argued that the penalties for sodomy under the *ancien régime* had been too harsh.[15] The Enlightenment thinkers' rational approach to punishment offered no grounds for punishing homosexual acts provided that they occurred between consenting individuals. In the words of Condorcet, "sodomy, when there is no violence involved, cannot be part of the criminal law; it does not violate the rights of anyone."[16] Yet it is hard to measure with precision the influence of these ideas on the Constituent Assembly that was in charge of drafting the Penal Code of 1791. Indeed, there is no indication that the Assembly even took the *philosophes'* opinions of sodomy into account, since "the legislators never provided any explanation for this omission, *which they never even debated.*"[17] Thus as Michael Sibalis suggests, "the decriminalization of sodomy was simply a fortuitous and unforeseen consequence of their secularization of criminal law."[18] At the very least, the ideas of the Enlightenment, "helped to open up the discursive space in which the traditional intolerance of same-sex sexuality could be contested, or at least quietly dropped."[19] The only possible reference to sodomy in the legislative debates of 1791 comes from Le Pelletier de Saint-Fargeau's explanation to the Constituent Assembly that the new penal code should outlaw only "true crimes" and not "those phony offenses, created by superstition, feudalism, the tax system, and despotism."[20] Crimes "created by superstition" undoubtedly referred to crimes originating in the Christian religion including blasphemy, heresy, sacrilege, and witchcraft, and also quite probably bestiality, incest, and sodomy. The vagueness of the term "crimes created by superstition" allowed Revolutionary legislators simply to pass over "in silence, acts that had once, at least in theory, merited the most severe penalties."[21]

Of course, the legislators' silence does not on its own indicate that the omission of the crime of sodomy was unintentional. Another possible interpretation is that in the minds of the legislators, sodomy remained of such a heinous character as to merit a certain degree of rhetorical modesty. Perhaps, they believed that an open discussion of the crime of sodomy would have offended prevailing moral sensibilities, and hence, should be referred to only obliquely during the legislative debates. In the end, the answer to the question of whether the legislative silence in 1791 was the result of modesty or accidental omission may be lost to history, but perhaps it does not matter which interpretation is valid, since they both support the same conclusion – neither the interpretation based on modesty nor the interpretation based on accidental omission can be used as evidence of an overt expression of tolerance of sodomy by lawmakers.

Sodomy was not the only crime left out of the Penal Code of 1791; in fact the only sex crime that remained in the code was rape – an indication perhaps that the legislators of 1791 considered matters of sexual morality to be generally outside the scope of the law.[22] The only other exception to the legislative silence with regard to sex crimes was a law from July 1791, enacted independently of the Penal Code that treated the issue of public indecency.[23] The legislative silence that began in 1791 continued until the end of the Napoleonic era; then in 1810, two new sexual crimes appeared in the French penal code: the crime of "sexual assault with violence of a child younger than fifteen years" (*attentat à la pudeur avec violence sur un enfant de moins de quinze ans*) and the crime of "corruption of minors" (*incitation habituelle de mineurs à la débauche*), which was generally understood as pimping minors for prostitution. The Penal Code of 1810 did not yet make any mention of "sexual assault without violence" – a crime that does not appear until 1832, when the age of sexual majority was set at eleven (raised to thirteen in 1863) – nor did it make any mention of sodomy.

One popular explanation for the omission of the crime of sodomy in 1810 is that it was the result of the efforts of one man: the jurist, Jean-Jacques Régis de Cambacérès, arch chancellor under Napoleon Bonaparte. He benefited from a powerful position under Napoleon, it is true. It is doubtful, however, that the exclusion of the crime of sodomy in the Penal Code of 1810 can be traced solely to Cambacérès's political and personal influence. For one thing, the crime of sodomy was first omitted in 1791, when he was still an unknown provincial judge.[24] With regard to the reforms of 1810, the confusion probably stems from the fact that Cambacérès did play an important role in the writing of the *Civil* Code of 1804 but did not participate in the drafting the Penal Code of 1810.[25]

### The Penal Code's silence regarding sodomy frustrates nineteenth-century police and judges

Evidence of a widespread desire to restrict homosexual acts comes from judges, police and legal scholars who called for stronger mechanisms for controlling homosexual activities. Given the prevalence of the desire to restrict homosexual acts and the moral climate under the Empire, which would have most likely welcomed the reinstatement of the crime of sodomy quite readily, the omission of the crime of sodomy in 1810 seems especially peculiar.

Between 1791 and the drafting of the Penal Code in 1810, judges from across France expressed frustration with the absence of a crime against sodomy. A case from 1794 illustrates this: two men, Etienne Rémy, a twenty-two-year-old soldier and Mallerange, a fifty-year-old civilian, were arrested on the Champs-Elysées after police found them half-naked and in a compromising position. At their trial, the judges of the Correctional Court of Paris decided that "in this case, it is a matter of knowing whether the accused were guilty of the crime against nature."[26] Their reference to the "crime against nature" indicates that these judges were unaware that the crime of sodomy had been abolished in 1791. The court later corrected itself and issued a final verdict based on criminal laws in force at the time, specifically, the law against public indecency. When the case was appealed, the judges were shocked to discover that the Penal Code did not mention sodomy. In the end, they agreed with the lower court that Mallerange's and Rémy's actions fell under the public indecency law of 1791, even though they imagined that the omission of the crime of sodomy could only be explained by the "horror inspired by the crime," which would have prevented legislators from talking openly about it.[27] Judges from other courts agreed. That same year for example, a judge from a criminal court in Indre declared that "crimes against nature so revolt the mind, that one can hardly believe in their existence … should not these sorts of crimes be classed among offenses in the Penal Code?"[28]

Members of the police force vocalized their revulsion for homosexual practices as well. In 1798, Police commissioner Picquenard wrote a letter to Merlin de Douai, President of the Executive Directory stating that "pederasts have established themselves [in Paris] … Citizen President, criminal laws are lacking for these sorts of crimes. These notorious crimes have not been articulated clearly enough, thereby hindering courts and assuring that the guilty remain unpunished."[29] The executive branch of the government also expressed its opinion for the need to restrict homosexual acts; and in 1805, the issue of sodomy even reached Napoleon who was called upon for an authoritative decision on the issue of whether the law against public indecency from 1791 could be interpreted to proscribe homosexual acts more generally. Napoleon, referred the question to Jérôme Guillard, the imperial prosecutor for the department of Eure-et-Loir, who was shocked that "our new laws have, as some people seem to think, remained silent on [sodomy]."[30] He recognized that the crime did not appear in the Penal Code but assumed that the code's silence was due to the prudishness of the Constituent Assembly, which "perhaps out of respect for public decency... did not want to set down the horrible name [of the crime] in black and white."[31] Napoleon was the ultimate arbiter for the issue, and though he expressed his extreme dislike for homosexual practices, he insisted that the law preserve its silence with regard to sodomy: "We are not in a country where the law should concern itself with these offenses. Nature has seen to it that they are not frequent. The scandal of legal proceedings would only tend to multiply them."[32]

Legal scholars were no more tolerant of homosexual acts than judges and police, as is apparent in the language of a legal dictionary of the 1830s: "The various acts that we have just reviewed, however shameful and culpable they may be, no longer appear in our penal legislation... Moreover, can justice prosecute them without danger?... What good would it do to unmask so many hidden depravities, so many shameful mysteries? Does morality benefit from these vile revelations?"[33] Now this context of a widespread desire to restrict homosexual practices raises an obvious question: If so many authorities were in agreement over the desire to restrict homosexual acts, what prevented nineteenth-century legislators from simply reinstating the crime of sodomy? To answer this, it is important to recall that the various forms of sexual control available in the nineteenth century (sexual assault with violence, public indecency, sexual acts with minors, and procuring minors for prostitution) went no further than penalizing crimes with ascertainable victims. Legislators seem to have recognized that sodomy (defined as sexual acts between consenting adults in private) was a victimless crime, which could not be penalized without violating basic principles of the French legal system. This wisdom on the part of lawmakers was attributable at least in part to "their attachment to the rationalist principles inherited from eighteenth-century philosophy, which permeated the entire code of 1810."[34] In this way, the same rationalist values that inspired the republican Penal Code of 1791 made repression of "other kinds of perversion utterly impossible in 1810 beyond those... that were legitimized by the use of violence."[35]

## The incompatibility of French universalism and victimless crimes

In all liberal legal systems a fundamental principle requires that every crime have a victim. This principle may be restated in different forms, for example: one's own liberty ends once it begins to infringe upon the liberty of another. Or in the words of the famous eighteenth-century French legal scholar Jean-Étienne-Marie Portalis, "When all individuals can do whatever they please, they may do things that disturb others, they may do things that disturb a great number of people. The freedom of particular individuals would inevitably lead to the suffering of all. It is necessary therefore to have laws to direct actions."[36] This idea that a particular activity can only be prohibited if it harms another is the basis for the requirement that every crime must have an ascertainable victim.

For some crimes, the victims are of course relatively artificial legal creations. For example in France, duels have been forbidden between two consenting individuals since the sixteenth century (Henri II's death in a duel in 1559 brought about the first law against duels), where the victim created through French legal scholars' writings on the topic was the public, and in particular, women, who would have had to witness the duel's violence. In fact, the "public" is frequently cited as the victim of crimes for which it is not obvious who the victim would otherwise be. In recent decades, the state has extended the notion of victim by claiming the right to limit individual freedom in the interest of public health through laws requiring seat belt use, for example. However, with regard to sexual acts in private between consenting adults, the determination of the victim becomes problematic. So why is it that France managed to keep homosexual acts legal while other liberal democracies like the United States continued to criminalize them?[37]

After the French Revolution, the nascent Republic found inspiration for the structure and general principles of its new legal system not in the legal precedents of the *ancien régime* but in the writings of jurists of the Bologna School from the eleventh century who had resuscitated the ancient Justinian code of the Roman Empire. Consequently, as the product of academics, the French legal system has been characterized primarily by its extremely rational or "artificial" nature, striving for universality of principles and a high level of coherency among its various provisions. Portalis explained that "Laws are not purely acts of power, they are acts of wisdom, of justice and of reason."[38] The need for coherency, rationality, and *universality* of principles makes it particularly difficult for the republican legal system to accommodate exceptions to general principles such as the requirement that every crime must have a victim.

If the French legal system's need for coherency and universality of principles is considered remarkably strong in comparison to the legal systems of most liberal democracies, than legal systems like the common law systems of the United States or of England can be seen as representing the opposite end of the continuum. These systems have arisen from a series of historical precedents, and in this way, they are characterized by a relatively "organic" evolution and by their respect for tradition. Like the French system, these systems also rely on certain fundamental principles; however, they are different from the French system in that they can more easily accommodate exceptions to general principles, particularly when such exceptions arise from a long respected tradition. American anti-sodomy laws are a good example of such an exception. In 1962, the developers of the American *Model Penal Code* explicitly recognized that sodomy laws violated the principle that every crime must have a victim by asserting that for the crime of sodomy it is acceptable to sacrifice "personal liberty, not because the actor's conduct results in harm to another citizen but only because it is inconsistent with the majoritarian notion of acceptable behavior."[39] In the famous 1986 American case concerned with the issue of the constitutionality of sodomy, *Bowers v. Hardwick*,[40] the Supreme Court heard arguments, some arguing that sodomy laws violated the principle that every crime have a victim, and others responding that the long tradition of criminalizing sodomy, which dates at least as far back as medieval England, justified an exception to this general principle: "Proscriptions against that conduct have ancient roots ... Sodomy was a criminal offense at common law and was forbidden by the laws of the original thirteen states when they ratified the Bill of Rights."[41] Justice Burger added that "decisions of individuals relating to homosexual conduct have been subject to state intervention throughout the history of Western civilization ... To hold that the act of homosexual sodomy is somehow protected as a fundamental right would be to cast aside millennia of moral teaching."[42]

In this way, the historical origins of the French legal system help explain why in the early days of France's First Republic it would have been especially difficult to forbid sexual acts between consenting adults, since such a law would have presented an exception to the general liberal principle that every crime must have a victim, and in the context of universalist France, exceptions to such basic principles would have been nearly impossible to make. As the French legal scholar, Jean Danet, points out: "Laws are understood to punish only when there are victims. Individuals 'forced' to witness a sexual act, or victims of physical violence exercised toward sexual ends legitimized punishment. Any other pleasure or perversion remained outside the scope of penalization so long as it was consented to by all parties concerned."[43] The universalist spirit of the First Republic's Penal Code of 1791 carried through the various regimes of the nineteenth century up to the present day, protecting individuals who engaged in same-sex sexual acts from the kinds of harsh treatment seen in other European countries (except for a few countries, such as the Netherlands in 1811, that adopted the French Penal Code after having it imposed on them by French revolutionary and imperial armies).

The decriminalization of homosexuality in France protected French homosexuals to an extent, but not entirely. Nineteenth-century police and judges were able to use the existing nondiscriminatory laws, especially the law on public indecency, in discriminatory ways. Louis Canler, a police official from the July Monarchy, explained in his memoirs that the discriminatory treatment of homosexuals was justified because of their alleged connection to the criminal under-world – the idea being that surveillance of homosexuality would ultimately lead to fewer thefts of private property.[44] Surveillance efforts increased in the decades following. Félix Carlier, who was head of the vice police for the Paris prefecture in the 1860s, reveals that "from 1860 to 1870, the repression was so severe that there were moments of true panic [among homosexuals]."[45] He adds that,

> In general, pederasts tremble in the face of public opinion. [But] they are only cynical with each other. In their dance parties, in their private meetings, they push this cynicism to an unheard of degree. You would think that you were in a group of drunk call girls during a night of orgies... [but] when those people are no longer in their own environment... they show timidity up to the point of cowardice; they whose audacity at times is without limits. Instead of defending themselves, they run. Then through anonymous letters [of denunciation], they take revenge against each other.[46]

Through exceptional attention to details, these anonymous letters of denunciation often display too much knowledge on the part of their authors for them to escape suspicion themselves.[47] This explains why, in an effort to preserve anonymity, these letters were almost always written in capital letters with childlike script. These denunciations serve as evidence of a widespread knowledge of the legal requirements for police repression of homosexuality, and in particular, the requirement that the sexual act in question be conducted in public. For example, a letter from October 1879 describing homosexual acts that had taken place in the public urinals at the *Place des Petits Pères* in Paris focused on how the acts were capable of harming the general public, arguing that the acts perpetrated at the urinals, which were out of view, produced sounds that could nonetheless be heard from outside.[48] This letter was in fact successful in leading to the arrest of ten people several days later.[49] The general awareness of the legal requirements and of the possibility for discriminatory police enforcement, as shown by these letters is evidence of a shared fear on the part of Paris homosexuals during this period; a fear which manifested itself in the (self-?)denunciations of the time. A cycle established itself, by which denunciations allowed for increased police repression, which escalated fears and gave rise to more letters. Thus as William Peniston has pointed out, "despite the decriminalization in the penal codes, same-sex sexual behavior became increasingly criminalized, at least in the practices of the police."[50]

This is not to say that homosexuality went into the closet during this time. On the contrary, a vibrant homosexual subculture for both men and women developed during the last decades of the nineteenth century, particularly in the central *arrondissements* of Paris, complete with its own cultural codes and places to socialize. At the end of the century, gay male communities and lesbian communities overlapped to a large extent and shared "many neighborhoods and institutions, from Montmartre...to the brothel (gay or otherwise), the theater, the masked ball, the *brasserie*, and the dance hall."[51] Meanwhile, the areas where only men cruised one another included the many new outdoor spaces and the *grands boulevards* that came along with the Haussmannization of the city. The accompanying commercial revolution led to the creation of new luxury shops, which provided covered arcades in front of the city's new luxury shops where "the objects for sale included not only material things, but human beings as well."[52] According to Régis Ravenin's study, in addition to these public spaces, men could meet one another in at least 110 commercial establishments all over Paris with a somewhat higher density in the second and ninth arrondissements.[53] These meeting spaces did not go unnoticed, however, and the increased visibility of homosexuality led to calls for increased surveillance. In the context of the homosexual community of Paris at the end of the nineteenth century, the mechanisms of control existed as much through external police repression as through internalized mechanisms of self-control. Power exercised in the form of self-control or auto-censure is an important aspect of Foucault's assertion that power is "dispersed through the network of relationships which make up society and based in discourse...that it is not exercised in a single, downward vector."[54] Dispersed power and its reliance on mechanisms of self-control appears as the most appropriate lens through which the policing of the Parisian homosexual "community" of the *Belle Epoque* can be examined.

"*Pédéraste*" rather than "*homosexuel*" was the term used in the police reports of the latter half of the nineteenth century. The word *pédéraste*, however, almost never takes on the meaning of sexual acts between male youth and male adults in these reports. An example of this use of the word *pédéraste* in reference to same-sex acts between adults can be found in a series of police reports from April of 1865,[55] dealing with the investigation of a certain Monsieur Cabanier, a knight of the Imperial Guard, described as "a man from the South, a handsome young man with a husky voice."[56] These documents were produced for a trial for the removal of Cabanier from the Imperial

Guard on the grounds of homosexual activities conducted in private. Homosexual members of the military had more to fear during that time than civilians, because homosexual acts, even when conducted in private, could bring on investigations leading toward expulsion from the military. The need for secrecy gave rise to special meeting spaces for homosexual members of the military that were sheltered from public view.

Cabanier frequented some of these spaces, in particular, the Hôtel de l'Alma (situated in the old Passage de l'Alma on the left bank), the Taverne Anglaise, and the military parties at the Ecole Militaire's Salon de Mars – three key spots in the cartography of military men's homosexual activities during this time.[57] The police reports state that Monsieur Cabanier "had [sexual] relations with other *pédérastes* who were known by women's names;"[58] that he "often came to the Hôtel de l'Alma, and that in asking about the civilian *pédérastes* who frequented that place, he would often say: 'Isn't there a single one here tonight?' "[59] The police reports conclude with the words "Cabanier is a *pédéraste*."[60] In these reports, and indeed, in others of the time, the use of the term *pédéraste* is clearly not intended to refer to sexual acts between adults and youth. However, it is not clear to what degree connotations of pederasty might have nonetheless continued to resonate with the word *pédéraste* during this time.

Among the documents for Cabanier's trial, the oral testimony of a certain Louise Ferrand, a twenty-three-year-old prostitute who also frequented the Hôtel de l'Alma, provides a particularly informative indicator of the construction of sexual identities from the time.[61] Cabanier claimed before the military tribunal that he had had sexual relations with Ferrand. According to his testimony, it seems that this single fact could alone serve as evidence of his heterosexuality, and consequently, of the impossibility of his having participated in homosexual acts.[62] What is more surprising, perhaps, is that the military tribunal focused its attention on this defense and on an examination of the relations between Cabanier and Ferrand. Ferrand claims in her oral testimony, however, that she and Cabanier never had sexual relations:[63]

Here are the circumstances: a certain Monsieur Emile d'Orléans, a well known *pédéraste* at the Hôtel de l'Alma had invited Cabanier to walk around with him for the whole day and to avoid suspicion, he asked me to join the group – Emile took care of paying for everything that day and in evening when he took us to the Taverne Anglaise, a meeting spot for *pédérastes*. We went back to the Hotel around one o'clock in the morning, and since Emile didn't want to stay over, and moreover, since my room was the only one free and it was too late to go back where we came from, Cabanier slept with me, but in all innocence and honor.[64]

Through its extensive examination of the possibility for sexual relations between Ferrand and Cabanier, the military tribunal makes apparent its assumption that homosexual and heterosexual desires could not coexist within a single person. This understanding of a fixed sexual orientation, as either entirely heterosexual or homosexual, is quite different from older models of sexual categorization, going back as far perhaps as ancient Greece, if not further, which assumed that a single person was capable of both heterosexual and homosexual acts. In this way, these documents from 1865 serve as evidence that an understanding of sexual orientation resembling that of contemporary gays and lesbians (that is, as a comprehensive and invariable sexual identity) already seems to have been established by the second half of the nineteenth century.

## Nineteenth-century medical "experts" identify two of sodomy's victims: the public and youth

The police's interest in monitoring homosexuals in the latter half of the nineteenth century coincides with an increased reliance on medical "experts," whose studies would eventually lay the groundwork for future legal control by explicitly identifying two potential victims of homosexuality: the "public" and "youth." By the beginning of the Third Republic, a veritable medico-criminological science was beginning to take shape. Perhaps, French society was looking for new moral guidance in the form of scientific clerics to replace the old moral order's direction, and found guidance in the new "experts" of morphology, phrenology, psychiatry, and medico-criminology. The most famous doctor in this field was Ambroise Tardieu who explained that

The characteristic signs of passive *pédérastie*, which we will look at in succession, are the excessive development of the buttocks, the

infundibular (funnel-shaped) deformation of the anus, the relax-
ation of the sphincter... It is on the virile member that we expect
to find the mark of active habits. The dimensions of the penis on
individuals who participate as the active partner in sodomy are
either very spindly or very voluminous: slenderness is the general
rule, fatness is the rare exception; but in all cases, the dimensions
are excessive in one direction or the other...[65]

At the end of his extensive report on the supposed physical characteristics of homosexuals, Tardieu explained that his purpose was
to give "to the expert medical witness the means to recognize pederasts by certain signs, and thus, to resolve with greater certainty and
authority than has been possible up to the present, the questions
for which justice invokes his assistance in order to pursue and, if
possible, eradicate this disgraceful vice."[66] Indeed, with the developing notions of contagion tied to the Pasteurian revolution, medical
reports like Tardieu's began to place the emphasis on the dangers
homosexuality might pose to "public order." And in 1895, Doctor
Paul Garnier published a study that focused solely on the case of fet-
ishist homosexuals, and in particular, the fetish for polished leather
boots, which stated this thesis quite clearly. In the general conclusion to his study, Garnier explains that "the moral troubles resulting
from such obsessions is such that they remove one's capacity for self-
control. Consequently, it is in the interest of both the person charged
and of public order to put him under the control of an administra-
tive authority in order to place him in an insane asylum."[67]
Though the majority of these medial studies were concerned with
male homosexuality, nineteenth-century sexologists did not ignore
lesbians. Like their studies of male homosexuals, the studies of lesbians blamed many cases of female homosexuality on an individual's
vulnerability to contagion when faced with broader social changes.
As Gretchen Schultz has pointed out in her recent study of representations of fin-de-siècle lesbianism, the spread of female homosexuality was attributed to the existence of all-female spaces, which were
"presumed to be breeding-grounds for lesbianism, be they prisons,
brothels, boarding schools, or convents," but was also strongly associated with the "changing roles and growing liberties of women (such
as increased access to education and growing numbers of women in
the work force resulting in greater independence from men)..."[68]

Collectively, these medicolegal experts' testimonies of male and female homosexuality and the effort they made to couch the dangers of homosexuality in terms of its threat to the public (either through notions of contagion or through the threat posed to "public order") served to establish a victim in this context. This particular line of reasoning, through a reliance on the potential harm done to the victim constructed in the form of the "public," was articulated with greater precision as the nineteenth century drew to a close, and by the interwar period, the notion that there might be certain situations where homosexuality would not be a victimless crime had become well ingrained in political discourse.

After the First World War, homosexuality was blamed for the alleged social weaknesses responsible for France's defeat, though as Carolyn Dean points out "it is never clear in these attacks whether homosexuality was the cause or symptom of the war...but in every instance, homosexuality reenacted the trauma of war as the experience of spectacularly degraded manhood."[69] Nineteenth-century fears of contagion were heightened during the interwar period, as social commentators began to recognize that homosexuals were not so easily identified, that even seemingly masculine men or feminine women could be susceptible to homosexual desires, that the "disease" of homosexuality could spread through French society silently and invisibly. The medical experts' testimonies from the nineteenth century that enumerated identifying characteristics of homosexuality became increasingly discredited, which meant that homosexuality might be much more widespread than had been previously imagined and could be spreading undetected, making it nearly impossible to control or limit. Young men during the "fragile" years of adolescence were considered to be particularly susceptible to contamination from older homosexuals.[70] As one doctor put it in the 1930s, "how many little boys have become homosexual because of the candy offered by a handsome gentleman encountered one day at the end of school?"[71]

Somewhat paradoxically, fears of the invisible spread of the disease of homosexuality coincided with an increased visibility of the homosexual scene in the interwar period. In the 1920s, it was possible to find specialized bars and homosexuals began to feel safe even if the sense of security was to a large extent illusory.[72] Also, in 1924, French homosexuals produced their first journal, *Inversions dans l'art, la littérature, l'histoire, la philosophie et la science* (the name was changed to *Amitié* in 1925). The editors of *Inversions* made it clear that the French homosexual community was not to be understood as a subculture trying to gain access to the dominant culture, but rather as "a society within society." The idea was that homosexuals already occupied important positions in society and the journal's mission was merely to expose this reality. *Inversions* was the first journal of its kind, aimed specifically toward homosexuals, yet sold openly in a number of Parisian kiosks. The words "in art, literature, history, philosophy and science" in the title made it clear that the journal's strategy was to emphasize the contributions homosexuals have made to these socially recognizable pillars of knowledge throughout history, to emphasize a connection between homosexuality and production of high culture, to assert that it was not at all a question of bringing homosexuals into high culture because they were already there.

Between the pages of an issue of *Inversions*, one was sure to find at least one article that "outed" a celebrated writer, such as Shakespeare or Goethe. The underlying assumption was not just that homosexuality had been practiced by many of history's greatest figures, but also that there seemed to exist a link between homosexuality and creative genius: "Should homosexuals be considered abnormal? If we consider an intellectual, a poet or a genius abnormal, I would accept that the homosexual is an abnormal being... But through some strangeness of nature, these are the same beings who are inclined toward homosexuality. Is there a direct link between homosexuality and genius?"[73] Articles legitimized homosexuality also through references to classic antiquity and to more contemporary writers such as Oscar Wilde, André Gide, or Walt Whitman. Despite the fact that the editors were not themselves men of letters and that none of the more famous homosexuals writers of the period ever contributed to the journal, writers maintained a seemingly forced tone of cultivated civility and simulated erudition. The aim of *Inversions* was not to assert difference or to claim that homosexuals should be treated as equals despite their difference, but rather to claim that homosexuals were already assimilated, not just into society at large but into the most prestigious spaces of high French culture: "Now, all or almost all great men, the most creative men, the most generous men and the most fertile men, have loved Ganymede rather than the vulgar Venus."[74]

Yet despite this increased visibility associated with presence of specialized bars and with a journal like *Inversions*, homosexual political movements like those seen in Germany and in Britain at the time did not form during the interwar period in France. This had to do with the relative legal tolerance in France, but also with what Florence Tamagne refers to as "the individualism of French homosexuals," who tended to shun the idea of belonging to associations.[75] As a result, the public's image of homosexuality was constructed not so much by homosexuals themselves, but by police and by doctors, who portrayed homosexuals as criminals and as potential traitors to the French nation. The growing association of homosexuality with moral decadence, with notions of contagion, and with the alleged weakness of France's men after the war led to even greater calls on government officials to do something to stop its spread. These fears, on the eve of the Second World War, required action, symbolic or real, on the part of the government. This historical context and also the growing perception that homosexuality might indeed have its victims – either in the form of youth through contagion or the public through the threats it allegedly posed to public order or national security – set the stage for legal action. It was therefore not a chance event when in 1942, a law responding to these fears – the first to discriminate explicitly between homosexual and heterosexual acts since 1791 – was signed and promulgated by the Marshal Philippe Pétain.

# 1
# It Could Have Been Worse
# (1940s–1960s)

Today, it is from yourselves that I wish to save you.[1]

Maréchal Philippe Pétain (August, 1941)

In 1942, France's legal silence with regard to homosexuality came abruptly to an end. As head of the collaborationist Vichy government, Philippe Pétain signed a law establishing separate ages of sexual majority for homosexuals and heterosexuals – for homosexuals the age was raised to twenty-one, while for heterosexuals the age remained thirteen.

The fact that this law was concerned with the issue of sexual majority might be interpreted on its face as the sign of a widespread association of male homosexuality with either pederasty (sex between an adult male and an adolescent boy) or pedophilia (sex between an adult and a prepubescent child). These associations certainly existed in lawmakers' heads, but there are a couple of problems with assuming that they alone inspired the 1942 text: First, it is problematic to speak of French "lawmakers" with respect to the 1942 law, since the law was enacted under the particular circumstances of the Vichy government in August 1942, a time when Pétain could sign laws into existence without legislative review. After the war, in 1945, the law was preserved in the French Penal Code not through legislative review but by way of ordinance, which means that once again there was no legislative debate. Second, the original motivation for the law's creation was most likely not fully reflected in the resulting law's text. The conservative discourse of Vichy and in particular, Vichy's promotion of traditional family and gender roles, suggests that homosexuality in general would have been under attack, not just relations between adults and minors. Indeed, documents produced in the years prior to 1942 indicate that there was a desire among high-level ministers to criminalize homosexuality altogether, but also an awareness of why it would be difficult to do so. The fact that the law did not go further is a sign of the persistence of certain values normally associated with the French republican legal system, even in the context of Vichy.

A second discriminatory law appeared in 1960 that doubled the penalty for public indecency when the acts were between people of the same sex. This law can also be interpreted differently depending on whether one gleans its meaning through an isolated reading of the law's text or whether one considers the law in a broader context. The 1960 law concerns itself with the crime of public indecency, and from this alone it would be easy to conclude that it resulted from a simple association of homosexuality with public sex. However, for reasons similar to those offered for the 1942 law, this kind of reading of the 1960 law is potentially misleading, since the specific target of the 1960 law was chosen at least in part because it satisfies the republican legal system's need for this crime to have a victim. Like for the 1942 law, the impetus for the 1960 law could have begun with a desire to restrict all homosexual acts without having the legal license to do so. Together, these two laws demonstrate how the limits of the French republican legal system ultimately helped French homosexuals escape more severe forms of legal repression.

## The 1942 law locates its victim: "youth"

On August 6, 1942, Marshal Pétain signed a law adding a new line to Article 334 of the French Penal Code punishing anyone who "commits one or more lewd acts or acts against nature with a minor of one's own sex below the age of twenty-one in order to satisfy his or her own passions" with six months to three years of prison along with a fine of 2,000 to 6,000 francs.[2]

After the Liberation, many of the most offensive laws of Vichy, such as those affecting the status of Jews, were eliminated from the French legal codes, yet others, especially those that had to do with the family along with those like the 1942 law that had to do with "public morality," remained. In the context of postwar France this might not be so surprising. Recently, historians have emphasized "the continuities between Vichy and post-Liberation France, and the history of homosexuality offers no exception. ... Pro-natalist discourse was omnipresent in 1945 as part of the project to rebuild French influence in the world. De Gaulle made a speech calling for twelve million *'beaux bébés'* in the next ten years."[3]

Immediately following the war, legal scholars did not dispute the 1942 law's validity, but merely argued that the law had been "clumsily misplaced" in Article 334 of the Penal Code.[4] In 1945, this led to its being moved to Article 331, which contains provisions related to the protection of minors, while Article 334 treats "public nuisances" such as prostitution and "debauchery." The logic behind the resituating of the law is clear. Beginning in 1945, the crimes were categorized by *victim*: those for which the public was the victim belonged in Article 334, while those where minors were considered the victims were to be located in Article 331. The relocated provision maintained the age of sexual majority for homosexuals at twenty-one, while a second ordinance from July 1945 set the age of sexual majority for heterosexuals at fifteen.[5]

The relocation to Article 331 was done by ordinance under France's postwar provisional government without any legislative debate or explanation beyond a short clarification at the end of the law's text: "This reform inspired by the concern for preventing the corruption of minors, cannot in principle stir any criticism. But by its form, such a law would be better situated in Article 331."[6] Only one rather insignificant change was made to the 1942 law until its repeal in 1982: in 1974, the age of sexual majority for homosexuals was lowered to eighteen as part of a broader legal reform that changed the age of civil majority from twenty-one to eighteen across the board in all the Civil Code's and Penal Code's provisions.[7] With this modification, the 1942 law remained on the books without further changes until August of 1982.

The 1942 law should not appear shocking, given the general legal context of the Vichy government. Several months earlier, in December 1941, the law on the status of Jews had been promulgated and the 1942 law "arises from the same preoccupation: to atone for the errors of a country facing divine wrath, to designate the categories of the population responsible for the defeat."[8] Vichy's motto of "Work, Family, and Homeland" is, of course, an obvious indicator of the strict moral climate of the time. The association of homosexuality with moral decadence and "cosmopolitanism" had become a prevalent feature of European society in the 1930s, and in France this connection was particularly strong. The French, who were facing another humiliating defeat by the Germans not unlike the defeat of 1870, had begun to look inward for sources of weakness, and homosexuals, as alleged purveyors of moral decay in the 1920s and 1930s, became ideal scapegoats. The belief that French homosexuals might feel less allegiance to their fellow Frenchmen than to their homosexual "brothers and sisters" in the gay capital of Berlin was used as evidence of their potential for treason – indeed one term for homosexuality during this time was the "German vice."[9] These kinds of accusations, made in a context of growing nationalism, were of course also made against communists and Jews using a similar kind of propagandistic anticosmopolitanism.[10]

Another suspected source of French weakness was the low birth rate caused by the tremendous loss of young men's lives in the First World War. The powerful demographic concerns of the interwar period fueled public sentiment against homosexuals, who were seen as lacking in civic loyalty, because they were not producing French children. Certainly French political actors of the late 1930s were aware of the existence of the German Penal Code's infamous Paragraph 175, which criminalized homosexual relations between consenting adults, and which could have served as an inspiration for antihomosexual legislation in France. Yet, even in the context of Vichy, France did not produce a law restricting all homosexual acts. What stopped Vichy's high-level ministers from doing more? A look at the origins of the 1942 law sheds some light on the question.

## Origins of the 1942 law

In May 1939, the Minister of Justice, Georges Bonnet, received a petition signed by twelve jurors asking him to do something about homosexual prostitution in Paris. They had just participated in the trial of sixteen-year-old Roger Neuville. Neuville frequented establishments such as the "Kermesse Clichy" and the "Palais Berlitz;" places where young men went to meet older men who would pay them for sex. One night, Neuville met Maurice Rabouin, went home with him, spent the night with him, and killed him the next morning.

In their letter, the jurors asked for increased police surveillance of homosexual establishments in order "to prevent a recurrence of dramas as unfortunate as the one we just judged," and expressed their desire for a new law that would punish the solicitation of minors severely.[11] At the time, four laws made up the entire arsenal of what could be used against homosexuals: (1) the crime of sexual assault with violence (*Attentat à la pudeur avec violence*), (2) sexual assault without violence on a child younger than thirteen (*Attentat à la pudeur sans violence sur un enfant de moins de treize ans*), (3) public indecency (*outrage public à la pudeur*), and (4) corruption of minors under the age of twenty-one (*Incitation habituelle de mineurs au dessous de vingt-et-un ans à la débauche*), which was generally understood by courts to mean serving as a pimp for the prostitution of minors. In the case of Rabouin and Neuville, the jurors were dismayed to discover that the sexual transaction between the two men did not fit any of the four categories listed above, which meant that their sexual acts had been entirely legal.

The jurors' letter led to the commissioning of a report by M. Médan, the deputy public prosecutor for the Court of Appeals in Paris. Médan advocated adding a line to the Penal Code that would punish anyone who "commits one or more lewd acts against nature with a minor of one's own sex below the age of eighteen in order to satisfy his or her own passions."[12] This is most likely the earliest draft of what eventually would become the 1942 law – the only difference between it and the final text is the age mentioned, which was ultimately set at twenty-one.

This was not the first time that authorities had been called upon to do something. The French government already knew that men from the French navy were selling their bodies for sex and people like Georges Leygues, a minister of the navy, had been asking the government to do something about it since as early as the 1920s.[13] Reports from the French Ministry of the Interior in the late 1920s added that the "corrupters" of the marines were likely to be foreign, especially German, and since homosexuality was associated with pacifist and communist leanings, authorities feared that the spread of homosexuality could lead to a climate of insubordination and antimilitarism among French marines.[14]

The calls for legal reform circulating during the final years of the Third Republic survived the beginning of the Second World War and eventually made their way into the heads of Vichy's ministers. In 1941, a case involving a doctor who had sexual relations with teenage boy scout led to another report, where the formula originally devised by Médan in 1939 reappeared. In the report, Charles Dubost, the deputy public prosecutor of Toulon, criticized the Enlightenment thinking that contributed to the elimination of the crime of sodomy in the codes of 1791 and 1810:

> Under the influence of the *philosophes'* writings from the eighteenth century, the Empire's legislature, still full of revolutionary ideology, did not dare concern itself with the most repugnant of immoral acts. To do so would have gone against Rousseau's idea of man as naturally good ... [but also] against the right for individuals to lead their private lives however they wish, a right that they had just recognized and which must have caused the society's general interest to suffer terribly.[15]

Although he added that it might be useful to look at the methods other countries have used to prevent homosexuals from corrupting young men, including castration, which had "a favorable influence and could be adapted to our morals and beliefs," he ultimately recommended that the law be limited in scope to raising the age of sexual majority.[16] His suggested reform reproduces Médan's text almost verbatim – the only change is that the age was set at twenty-one.

Beginning in January 1942 and continuing through the spring, the Minister of Justice, Joseph Barthélémy worked on gaining support for the text that would eventually be signed by Pétain in August. Barthélémy was certainly interested in doing more than just raising the age of sexual majority. He shared Vichy's "concern with encouraging French people to have more children," but this had more to do with his "obsession with France's demographic weakness compared to Germany than with a desire to restore the ideal family" and thus sought to fight homosexuality for demographic reasons.[17]

In April 1942, Admiral François Darlan wrote a letter calling on the government to respond to "an important affair of homosexuality in which sailors and civilians have compromised themselves."[18] His frustration is evident when he explains that "current legislation does not allow any pursuit of the civilians, except in the case of public indecency."[19] He makes a plea for a law "that would allow for civilians and implicated members of the military to be pursued in the same way."[20] When Darlan wrote the letter on April 14, he was effectively second in command under Vichy, although just a few days later, on April 18, Pierre Laval would take his place. It is not entirely clear to what degree this letter motivated Pétain to sign the new law a few months later. The text had already been drafted before Darlan's letter arrived, yet it is easy to imagine that the letter may have been at least a motivating factor for Pétain to sign the law in August.

Now, to return to the original question: Why did the drafters of the 1942 Law respond to calls for broad restrictions of homosexual acts, like those from the twelve jurors in 1939 or those from officials in the French navy, with a law that only raised the age of sexual majority for homosexual acts? And if they chose to stop short of criminalizing all homosexuality, why did they choose to focus on the specific issue of the age of sexual majority?

It would be easier to assume that the authorities' main concern was to protect youth, had the drafters of the text kept the age set at eighteen. The decision to raise the age to twenty-one, however, suggests an intention to restrict homosexuality more broadly. The problem for the drafters of the text was that under French law, including the criminal law of Vichy, eighteen was recognized as the age of "discernment," so the logic used for protecting minors could no longer apply to those between the ages of eighteen and twenty-one. A new kind of logic was needed and it came in the form of establishing contagion as the vector through which homosexuality could be spread along with the desire to defend "public morality" and to eliminate perversion more broadly. As the legal scholar, Marc Boninchi, has pointed out, "the choice to criminalize acts with minors between eighteen and twenty-one had nothing to do with their protection, but with the imperatives of 'public morality' and a desire for the normalization of sexual practices."[21] Indeed, a report commissioned by the Ministry of Justice in March 1942 that supported raising the age explained that the age of eighteen is "not sufficient if one accepts that the protection that this text must offer is made not only in the personal interest of minors, but also in the interest of public morality."[22] At the end of the report, a handwritten addition from Henri Corvisy, the director of criminal affairs at the Ministry, suggested that Barthélémy consider "a more significant reform, returning to the principles of our old laws, which under the influence of Christian morality restricted adultery ... sodomy, incest and even bestiality and necrophilia."[23]

A few shared notions about homosexuality stand out in all the reports leading up to the 1942 law. It was widely accepted, for example, that the principal way by which one became homosexual was through contamination during the vulnerable years of adolescence. In all these documents, the descriptions of the young male prostitutes confirmed this by maintaining that before being contaminated by homosexuality, these young men were driven to have sex with other men purely out of financial desperation, and that they tried to maintain their virility by always performing the role of the insertive partner. In Médan's report, he explains that adult homosexuals are the truly guilty ones: "Without them, there would not be any young pederasts. Certainly there are very few inverts born that way."[24] Consequently, authorities realized that rather than trying to eliminate homosexuality in the adult population, the most efficient thing to do would be to go after the vector through which it allegedly spreads. Charles Dubost relied on this kind of reasoning in his report from 1941, where he suggested that even if it were possible to pass such a law that would apply to adults in private, it would not necessarily be the best way to control homosexuality:

> [Homosexuals] are only a social danger if they procure minors, because adults have little chance of being tempted or corrupted; and by openly pursuing a goal that can be taken care of by other more discrete and almost as radical methods, the law would unnecessarily attract attention to the sexual perversions it prohibits.[25]

Thus, to some degree it was out of concerns of practicality or efficiency that authorities failed to call for the criminalization of all homosexuality, but it is also clear from their reports that a minimal respect for certain republican values hindered calls for harsher legislation. For example, in his 1939 report, Médan alludes to the value of secularism when he explained that "there is no way this can be about making pederasty in general a crime... homosexuality is an issue of moral law, not penal law."[26] Similarly, Charles Dubost's report from 1941 makes it clear that it would certainly be desirable to punish all homosexual acts, but also lays out the reasons why it would be difficult to regulate sexual acts in private even in the context of Vichy: "I am not blind to the fact that such a radical measure would raise numerous objections. Some would worry about the invasion of privacy from police investigations of all kinds that would quickly become unbearable."[27] In the end, the authorities involved with the drafting of the 1942 law limited themselves to the specific issue of raising the age of sexual majority for practical reasons (the most efficient use of resources is to go after the vector by which homosexuality is allegedly transmitted; naming homosexuality in the law could attract unnecessary interest to the subject) but also out of minimal deference to republican values such as the requirement that every crime have a victim, the separation between religious and secular law, and the division between public and private spheres.

When Pétain signed the law in August, Barthélémy notified various navy admirals that action had been taken. One of them, Admiral Auphan who had already corresponded with Barthélémy several times during the drafting of the law, wrote back to explain that he thought the new law was an important first step, but was disappointed that the law did not go further. He asked the minister to "please examine the question of whether it would be possible to make homosexuality a crime," and pleaded with him to produce a law that would make "homosexuality on its own criminalized under penal law and punished by prison terms."[28] This letter, which was sent on November 9, 1942, was to be the last piece of correspondence between Barthélémy and Auphan. The next day, Germany violated its armistice agreement with Vichy and began its invasion of unoccupied France, and by the evening of November 11, German troops had reached the Mediterranean coast.

Until this point the cause of fighting homosexuality had been taken up at the highest levels by Darlan and Barthélémy, and if the government were going to do more to restrict homosexuality, it seems like the initiative would have had to come from one of these two men. However, as a result of the German invasions, neither of them would remain in their positions. Barthélémy's hostility to the new regime caused him to be increasingly isolated in the weeks that followed and he was eventually replaced by Maurice Gabolde in March 1943.[29] As for Darlan, he was assassinated in Algeria in December of 1942.

Had Barthélémy been able keep his position or had Darlan managed to stay alive, the minimal respect for republican values shown by the drafters of the law up to this point might not have withstood the pressure to take more extreme measures (of course even if Auphan's wish for a law criminalizing homosexuality in general had been realized, such a law would have most likely never been able to survive beyond the end of the war because of the restraints of the republican legal system that was put back into place after Vichy). Yet the fact that the events at the end of 1942 coincided with the end of the discussion of homosexuality among government officials in France raises an intriguing, ironic possibility: could it be that by a strange twist of fate, French homosexuals were saved from harsher treatment during the Second World War in part because of the German invasion of the *zone libre*?

## The 1942 law survives the end of the war

Earlier, it was mentioned that the relocation of the law in 1945 represented an effort to classify crimes by victim: those for which the "public" was cited as victim were to be found in Article 334, while those for which minors were victims were located in Article 331. This classification according to victim and more generally, the concern with ascertaining a victim for every crime in French law, is critical to understanding the motivation for preserving the 1942 law, just as it was central to interpreting the nineteenth century's legal silence.

A 1965 decision from the Correctional Tribunal of the Seine demonstrates the importance of making sure there is an identifiable victim for every crime in French law. In this case, the court sought to clarify the meaning of the word "with" in the 1942 law in the phrase "whoever shall commit a lewd act or an act against nature *with* a minor of the same sex."[30] In its decision, the court declared that: "If a minor voluntarily gives in to such acts...he must be considered a victim and not a guilty party."[31] French legal scholars had differing opinions on the validity of this court's interpretation. Michèle-Laure Rassat, disagreed with the court and argued that the presence of the term "with" in the 1942 law established the guilt of the minor, since generally speaking, the word "against" establishes the guilty party–victim link, while the word "with" creates a crime of accomplices.[32] Others, such as the legal scholar Jean Danet agreed with court's decision. In the end, it is not entirely clear whether the term "with" was included in the 1942 text by error or by Pétain's intention to make both the adult and the minor guilty parties. However, this is of little significance. What matters is the attention paid by the court, and by legal scholars to the issue of locating the victim here. In any event, it seems that the tribunal could not have concluded that the minor was an accomplice, even if the language of the text might indicate this, because by doing so the court would have effectively recognized a crime without a victim.

Clearly, things could have been worse. According to Jean Danet, in the years following the Second World War, "lawmakers had to give up the idea of condemning all homosexual acts, and so they chose a priority, the protection of minors; but fundamentally, it was homosexuality in general that was their focus."[33] The 1942 law is a much better outcome than what might have happened if the French Republic had been more lenient with regard to the requirement that every crime must have a victim. And though the law may have had important symbolic effects on the ways people thought about homosexuality at the time, its real effects were relatively inconsequential. In Paris, for example, the number of cases of "corruption of youth" was already decreasing prior to 1945, the year when the 1942 law first came into effect in Paris, and continued to decrease in the years immediately following the war (the average number of cases between 1928 and 1939 was 55 per year; between 1940 and 1944, 44.6 per year; and from 1945 to 1953, 33.8 per year).[34]

## The 1960 law locates its victim: "the public"

The history of the crime of public indecency goes back to the end of the eighteenth century. Since its creation in 1791, the crime has always consisted of three elements: an indecent act, a public context, and a guilty intention. Generally, "the indecent act can result only from attitudes or gestures: simple verbal assaults no matter how offensive cannot be considered indecent acts.... The most common cases are obscene exhibitions perpetrated by exhibitionists who expose their sexual parts in front of third parties."[35] As for the requirement of a public context, it is satisfied "not only in the case of immoral acts seen by one or more people, but also when, particularly by the nature of the place where it was committed, this act is offered for public view or when it might be seen even accidentally."[36]

In 1960, the law against public indecency was modified to punish homosexual acts more severely than heterosexual acts. The change was introduced into the Penal Code by the ordinance of November 25, 1960, a text aimed at controlling "social scourges," which eventually came to be known as the "Mirguet Amendment" in recognition of the French Deputy who proposed it, a deputy from the Moselle region, Paul Mirguet. Mirguet had respectable credentials – he had served in the French army during the 1930s and then was part of the French Resistance beginning in 1941 until the end of the war. When he was elected to the national assembly in 1958, he had run as a candidate of the newly formed Gaullist party, the Union for the New Republic.[37]

During the debates over the first draft of the law in July 1960, there was not yet any mention of homosexuality; the only "scourges" concerned were cancer, cardiovascular troubles, tuberculosis, alcoholism, and prostitution.[38] However, a few weeks later, during a second discussion of the law, Mirguet proposed the following amendment: "The Government is authorized to take by ordinance *all measures needed to fight against homosexuality*."[39] The scope of the authorization granted to the government by these words was excessively broad and vague, yet the parliamentary discussion of the amendment was surprisingly short. When it came time to discuss the amendment, Mirguet said, "I think that there is no use in drawing this out, because you are all aware of the gravity of the scourge that homosexuality represents, this scourge from which we have the duty to protect our children."[40] Compared to the extensive documentation of the origins of the 1942 law, there is little documentary evidence of the intentions behind this amendment. We are left only with Mirguet's short statement, which constitutes the entire discussion in the national assembly. No other justification was offered for the amendment and there was no debate over its merits. The record of the parliamentary debate merely adds that Mirguet's short statement was interrupted by laughs from the other deputies and by cries of "bravo!"[41] A vote was taken immediately and without any further discussion, his amendment was adopted almost unanimously.

The broad scope of Mirguet's amendment spawned fears among French homosexuals that the government might make homosexuality itself a crime. The most important homosexual organization of the time, *Arcadie,* responded to the amendment immediately with a letter addressed to Mirguet, which stated that "by asking the government to 'fight against homosexuality' without otherwise specifying your thoughts, you have opened the way for blind repression, for blackmailing, for neuroses, for the ruin of human lives."[42] As this letter indicates, the language of Mirguet's amendment was sufficiently vague that at the time one could easily imagine the government taking broad measures to restrict homosexuality.

Yet, when the government received authorization to take "all measures needed to fight against homosexuality," it did not exploit this authorization to its fullest, but rather chose to focus on the specific issue of public indecency by adding a new paragraph to Article 330 of the Penal Code. For heterosexual acts in public, the first paragraph of Article 330 applied, carrying a penalty of imprisonment for three months to two years and a fine of 500 to 4,500 francs. However, when the actors were of the same sex, the new second paragraph applied, approximately doubling the penalty for public indecency to six months to three years of imprisonment and a fine of 1,000 to 15,000 francs.[43] Mirguet must have been disappointed by the government's relatively weak response, since in his mind homosexuality represented a threat to the very survival of Western civilization. In an interview from 1975, he explained that above all he had hoped to protect minors but also to do something about the "'the falling birth rate' in the West, which he blamed in part on homosexuality. He predicted the Earth's population would grow to eight billion by AD 2000, but a shrinking proportion of these would be white, which means that 'our [European] civilization is doomed in the short term'."[44]

The broad language of the original authorization indicates that the legislators who voted for Mirguet's amendment would have accepted that the government go further than this, perhaps even forbidding all homosexual acts, including those conducted in private. Yet in the end, the government chose to concern itself only with the issue of public indecency. Why did the government show such restraint in this case? The 1960 law, like the 1942 law, seems to be the result of a compromise between the desire to restrict homosexuality more broadly and the need to respect the values of the French Republic, in particular, the requirement that every crime have a victim and the division between public and private spheres. It is difficult to make this assertion with complete certainty, since the government acted by ordinance, and thus, there are no documentary records of the discussion preceding the change to Article 330. The new Article 330 was discriminatory, certainly, but it did not violate the need for a victim, since the victim for the crime of public indecency had already been established as the "public," nor did it represent an invasion of privacy, since it only applied to acts in public spaces. By responding this way to the original authorization, the government was able to restrict homosexuality further, without violating the basic principles of the republican legal system.

In thinking about the decades following the Second World War in France, even with the 1942 law on sexuality majority and the 1960 law on public indecency on the books, it is easy to imagine that things could have been worse; and indeed, in other countries at the same time they were. In 1961, the legal scholar Marc Daniel wrote, "even since 1942, even since 1960, our antihomosexual legislation remains extremely liberal in spirit compared to many European countries, the United States or Canada. In fact, neither the Pétain law, nor the new Mirguet law has made homosexuality a crime, while any homosexual act is considered a crime in Great Britain, Germany, Austria, the United States, and Canada."[45] In this way, the 1960 law, just like the 1942 law, is an example of how the French republican legal system has limited the actions of lawmakers and allowed French homosexuals to be spared more extreme forms of legal repression.

## Living with dignity in the 1950s and 60s

The 1942 law on sexual majority and the 1960 law on public indecency both influenced the character of the political movements of the 1950s and 60s. Of the two, the 1942 law certainly had a greater influence, not only because homosexual political groups up through the 1970s tended to focus much more on its repeal, but also because members of these groups seem to have interiorized the association of male homosexuality with both pederasty (sex between an adult male and an adolescent boy) and pedophilia (sex between an adult and a prepubescent child), implicit messages of the 1942 law, and began to present this association with increased frequency in their representations of themselves.

In the 1950s, two groups served the political and social interests of (primarily male) homosexuals in France, and for both groups, the age of sexual majority was by far the most important issue. The first group, the *"Club Futur,"* began in 1952 and ended in 1955. The second and more important group, *"Arcadie,"* was founded in 1954 by André Baudry and continued to operate until 1982, although it is remembered mostly for its activities during the 1960s.

The *Club Futur*, began in conjunction with the first postwar homosexual review, *Futur*, which appeared in newsstands in October 1952. It was a politically engaged publication, "with a virulently anticlerical tone that preached sexual equality and repeatedly attacked ... advocates of family values and of the strict moral regulation of youth."[46] Couched in terms of liberating France's youth, *Futur*'s defense of pederasty was central to its political goals – in fact, the organization's members believed that the entire "repressive arsenal of the Penal Code pivot[ed] around the notion of sexual majority."[47] The journal's founder, Jean Thibault, apparently had a strong personal stake in this position, given that he and a friend had been found guilty of sexual relations with several teenage boys in July 1953.[48] Indeed, the journal was forced to close down to a large extent because of its constant criticism of the law establishing sexual majority. In April 1956, judges concluded that "by its virulent criticisms ... of the ordinance of 8 February 1945 [i.e., the 1942 law] ... *Futur* constitutes a danger to public morality and an offense against morals."[49] The publishers were charged with offending morals and were forced to cease publication.

Meanwhile *Arcadie*'s position with regard to the repeal of 1942 law and to the general issue of sex with minors was more complex. *Arcadie* strove for what André Baudry labeled "dignity," which in the words of Baudry meant that it was necessary "to educate adult homophiles, who too weak, and lacking knowledge, could not on their own live with dignity."[50] As many memoirs from the period have noted, the notion of dignity was central to the discourse of the *Arcadiens*. One such memoir published in July 1982 highlighted *Arcadie*'s call for dignity and provided a portrait of the man who began the French homophile movement, André Baudry: "Not a shadow of self-criticism nor of hesitation, no anxiety over perhaps having lost his way. He is right and the rest of the world is wrong, the world in general, and homosexuals in particular; for one last time, he becomes aggressive, he thunders: 'This world of permissiveness, of frivolity, of uncouthness – and the homophile people beat all records in this sad domain.' "[51] As for the political model of American homosexuals, he had nothing but contempt, as witnessed in this 1982 interview by *Gai pied* magazine: "*Gai pied:* Your opinion on American homosexuals? Baudry: I am disgusted enough by them to vomit. I pray to the gods of *Arcadie* that that will never reach France. Happiness, it must be said, is never found in excess."[52] A former member of *Arcadie* who knew Baudry personally, provided the following anecdote describing Baudry's character: "The main social activities of the *Club Arcadie* consisted of formal balls for men only. The orchestra would play and the men would dance together – however, if Baudry ever happened to see two men dancing too closely with each other, if ever two men dared to kiss each other in front of the others, Baudry would stop the orchestra's music, would point in their direction, and would order that they leave the ball immediately."[53]

An important element of Baudry's definition of dignity was its relatively apolitical stance. Generally, the *Arcadiens* did not allow themselves to protest openly against existing laws. With regard to political engagement, Baudry said that French homosexuals need to realize that "their problem is first and foremost a personal problem, and only second, a social problem. ... It is true that lawmakers have the duty to reconsider certain texts. But once more, that is not the main problem for homophiles. This is why *Arcadie* does not descend into these arenas where it would be all too happily devoured."[54] When the Mirguet amendment regarding public indecency passed in 1960, *Arcadie*, responded with a letter asking for clarification. Yet, it is difficult to interpret this letter as an indication of active political engagement on the part of *Arcadie*. The letter openly criticized the vague language of the amendment; however, with regard to controlling the less socially acceptable forms of homosexuality, *Arcadie* appears to be in complete agreement with Mirguet. The letter states, for example:

> Certainly, by asking parliament that the "fight against homosexuality" be included in the powers given to the Government, you mainly had in mind male prostitution ... Undoubtedly, you also thought of the shameful transvestites who dishonor certain cabarets, and of the indecent excesses found in certain boulevards and parks. And you were especially concerned with protecting children and youth from corruption. On all of these points, the great majority of French homosexuals, for whom we are the interpreters without any boastfulness nor false shame, agree with you.[55]

This excerpt is evidence of *Arcadie*'s particular political strategy, which involved distancing itself from the less palatable elements of male homosexuality, such as those found at the time in the neighborhood of Saint-Germain-des-Prés. Baudry had an especially strong disgust for men who lacked virility and was outspoken in his loathing of Saint-Germain, which was known for its *folles* "who stood out by their effeminate mannerisms, their swishing walk, their elegant clothes, sometimes their facial makeup, and especially their mannered way of speaking, often punctuated with piercing shrieks, which distinguished them from other homosexuals."[56] *Arcadie's* strategy of representing homosexuals as masculine, dignified, socially responsible individuals left room for only limited, relatively passive, political engagement. *Arcadie's* response to the 1942 law was similar to its response to Mirguet's amendment. Alongside its passive opposition to the discriminatory law governing the age of sexual majority, *Arcadie* often expressed a strong anti-pederastic position. Rather than openly combating the law, the *Club Arcadie* called on "pederasts to respect the law. Let's ask them even to suppress, through a new asceticism, their emotional and sexual orientation."[57] The anti-pederastic position taken by *Arcadie* was frequently the basis for tension between its members and the members of the *Club Futur* and eventually led to the two groups having nothing more to do with one another: "The director of *Arcadie*, affirms that at the beginning, the relations [with *Futur*] were courteous, [however], due to problems over the issue of minors, *Arcadie* will henceforth sever all relations."[58]

What is interesting is that despite Baudry's explicit disapproval of sex with minors, *Arcadie's* journal displayed a tremendous degree of interest in the subject of the age of sexual majority. Between 1954 and 1982, at least 38 articles appeared in the *Revue Arcadie* on the topics of pederasty and pedophilia (compared to only two articles written on the issue of public indecency, for example). These articles often mention the widespread association or confusion of male homosexuality with pederasty and pedophilia in France and demonstrate that for *Arcadie*, this association was an important obstacle facing "homophiles" on the road toward dignity: "The confusion of the noun, pederast, which is used by everyone to describe homosexuals, even by doctors, legal scholars, teachers, who mix up these two terms, should not happen among individuals who think of themselves as enlightened."[59] But not all the articles in *Arcadie* were critical of pederasty, particularly when the pederastic relationship was shrouded in allusions to classical Greece. In a 1997 interview, Gérard

Bach-Ignasse, a gay militant from the 70s, explained *Arcadie*'s relationship with the issue of pedophilia this way:

> I just spoke to a young researcher [who] said he couldn't understand how *Arcadie*, which talked so much about respectability, could at the same time talk so much about pedophilia. He just didn't understand, because now, the two things, homosexuality and pedophilia are completely separate, but back then, it wasn't the case... At the time, it was a way for *Arcadie* to be associated with these references from the high culture of Greece. Nowadays, that wouldn't work at all. People think very differently now... But any reference to classical Greece used to be considered a generally good one.[60]

Of course another reason for references to the high culture of classical Greece had to do with the constant threat of censure. After the government banned the sale of the magazine *Revue Arcadie* to minors in May 1954, Baudry recognized that he had to be cautious about what was published. In the years following, "the tone of its articles was serious and restrained, and its short stories were only discreetly erotic."[61] The tricky thing was that *Arcadie* had to offer a respectable public image and at the same time "attract readers who might be put off by its arid appearance."[62] The Review inserted an "additional mimeographed circular, which provided more specific information: a letter from the director, warnings about police surveillance or gay-bashing in cruising places, announcements of the group's cultural activities, and so on" for those who received the journal by subscription, in order to get around the risks of censure while still providing readers what they wanted (and as we will see in later chapters, the challenge of presenting a socially acceptable image of homosexuality while giving readers what they want was not specific to *Arcadie*, but rather, remains a feature of gay media in France).[63]

In interviews with former *Arcadie* members, the language they used to describe their memories of the period of the 1950s and 1960s was strikingly similar, appearing to have been strongly influenced by the *Arcadien* ideals, and notably, by Baudry's notion of dignity.[64] Grégoire,[65] a former member of *Arcadie*, had his first sexual relations around the age of twenty. All of his recent partners were self-reported as being with "mature" men, who were at least in their forties. He preferred to refer to the relationships he had with these men, not in terms of sexual relations, but as "literary, philosophical and artistic connections." He recalled that back in the 1950s, the idea of a stable, lifelong partnership with someone his own age was not part of his personal homosexual identity. He explained that the term "homosexual" was almost never used at that time, but rather the term "pederast" was the most commonly used term. He described homosexual pornographic magazines from the 1950s, which were printed mostly in the United States and whose pages were filled almost exclusively with photographs of boys, usually in their adolescence, but also frequently, in childhood (below the age of twelve, for example). According to Grégoire, there were no pornographic magazines at that time that displayed only photographs of adult men, like those available today. He described the issue of the age of sexual majority as "obviously the most important one" during that time. He is still bothered when young French people today invoke the slang term "pédé" to refer to homosexuals, because he imagines that one of the great developments in the 1980s was the construction of a homosexual identity that managed to distance itself from an association with pederasty or pedophilia.

Serge[66] was also a member of *Arcadie*. During the interview he seemed particularly concerned with the question of age. He spent most of the interview repeating that he was only interested in men his own age: "I like neither fruit which is too green, nor fruit which is too ripe." He spent a considerable amount of energy trying to convince me that his sexual tastes were uniquely for men of his own age. He answered questions about other issues as succinctly as possible, only to return the conversation each time to the issue of age, constantly reiterating the contempt he had for older men who looked for sexual partners among young boys or adolescents. He ended the interview by saying that he generally prefers to spend his time with "individuals who behave correctly and with dignity, in other words, not with queens or pedophiles."

From discussions with former members of *Arcadie*, but also from the general attention paid to the repeal of the 1942 law and the efforts made by early political organizations to distance male homosexuality from pederasty and pedophilia, it is clear that the issue of the age of sexual majority was of primary importance during the 1960s. Of the two laws, the 1942 law on sexual majority had a stronger influence on the shape of the first homosexual political movements appearing in the 1950s than the 1960 law on public indecency did; not only because these groups tended to focus much more on the repeal of the 1942 law than the 1960 law, but also because members of these groups seem to have at least partially interiorized the association of male homosexuality with pederasty and pedophilia.

In the end, it is difficult to evaluate the degree to which *Arcadie* helped or hindered French homosexuals of the time, since just like the Republic into which its members hoped to assimilate, *Arcadie* provided both protection and restraints. Homosexuals in the 1950s and 60s had "very different opinions of it ranging from unconditional support to pure and simple rejection. People afraid of having their homosexuality discovered and looking for no more than brief sexual encounters had no desire or need for *Arcadie*. But many others found moral comfort there."[67] Robert Francès who contributed to the review regularly remembers that "Arcadie was an institution that served on the one hand as a safeguard against possible mistakes and on the other as a moral savior."[68] Certainly for Robert Francès but also for many others like him, had *Arcadie* not existed or had French legislators been able to enact more restrictive laws, things could have been much worse.

# 2
# Attempts at Subversion (The 1970s)

> You say that society must integrate homosexuals, but I say that homosexuals must disintegrate society![1]
>
> Françoise d'Eaubonne, Winter 1970

It is widely claimed by contemporary French homosexual movements that the events of May 1968 brought about important changes in homosexual politics and lifestyles. This commonly shared understanding, however, could use some nuancing – it was not during the events themselves but in fact two or three years later that French homosexual politics rose up in the most radical and powerful forms ever witnessed until then and for that matter, since. Though "the libertarian atmosphere of May '68 might theoretically have opened up a space for sexual politics – making love *and* revolution, as the slogan had it – the immediate beneficiaries of the events were *gauchiste* groups like the Trotskyist *Ligue communiste* or the Maoist *Gauche prolétarienne* [who believed] that homosexuality was a bourgeois vice."[2] Jacques Girard, a gay militant and former member of the *Front homosexuel d'action révolutionnaire*, recalls that "in 68's concert of blaring horns, those of the homosexuals were not heard; however, when calm returned, a whispering could be heard, coming from over there, from the United States. In 1969, following the Christopher Street riots provoked by a police raid in the homosexual ghetto, the American Gay Liberation Front was born. [In France], there was a sigh of hope."[3]

The legal discriminations that had been put into place in 1942 and 1960 remained in force throughout this period, yet soon after the events of May, it became increasingly difficult to see the ways in which these legal discriminations continued to restrict the freedom of French homosexuals. On the contrary, it was during this period of maintained legal discriminations that the most radical forms of French homosexual political action ever witnessed appeared; and if one were to look only at laws, it would be easy to miss this critical rupture with the homosexual lifestyles and politics of the 50s and 60s. The 70s was a time when French homosexuals began to alter their strategies in fundamental ways, from a policy of *Arcadie*-style respectability and dignity to a new kind of in-your-face radicalism. In direct opposition to *Arcadie*'s strategy of embracing the republican model of integration by accepting French bourgeois norms as universally superior and by masking any glimmer of difference, the new political groups of the 70s placed value precisely on being *different* and on radically metamorphosing society as a whole. By the late 70s, however, it was clear that the anti-republican defense of radical difference had proved entirely incapable of producing legal change, and it was only after more assimilationist movements appeared in the late 70s that real change occurred. This recent chapter in the history of French gay politics serves as a reminder of what Enda McCaffrey has recently referred to as "the eternal capacity of the Republic to accommodate degrees of subversion but then always find a way to revert to type."[4]

The analysis of the political radicalism of the 70s brings up the question of what forms of political action are most effective in producing legal change in the context of republican France. In the 70s, political groups' radical demands, most notably, the elimination of an age of sexual majority altogether, proved entirely incapable of producing legal change. Strategies of compromise and accommodation were simply dismissed by homosexual militants of the time, which meant that the militants' demands were heard by society at large but not taken seriously. Moreover, it was not until the late 70s, and particularly with the creation of the more moderate and pragmatic *Comité d'urgence anti-répression homosexuelle* (the CUARH), that compromise became acceptable as a political strategy and that positive, legal change occurred.

Within a few years of the events of May '68, political mobilization of homosexuals reached its highest point ever witnessed in France. Not only were the numbers of new political militants on the rise, but the strength of their voices, the force of what they were saying and their presence in the media outside of the homosexual press caused French homosexuals to believe that they were living at the dawn of a new era, a time when *society as a whole* might be changed in the most fundamental and significant ways, a time when the possibilities for ever-increasing freedom seemed unbounded. This is not to say that the discriminatory laws were of no significance. While the number of arrests remained low through this period and the scope of the discriminatory laws focused only on public indecency and the age of sexual majority, the impact of these laws, in particular, the 1942 law, on the character of homosexual politics was substantial. To the extent that the 1942 law was concerned with the age of sexual majority, French political groups, in their struggle against this particular kind of discrimination, began to focus increasingly on the issue of youth sexuality. In this way, they, like their predecessors in the 1950s and 60s, accepted as axiomatic the common association of male homosexuality with pederasty and pedophilia, incorporating it into their strategies and their representations of themselves. What distinguished this new generation of militants from the homophiles of the previous decade though was that their political associations like the *Front homosexuel d'action révolutionnaire* and the *Groupes de libération homosexuelle* began to devote a considerable part of their efforts to *eliminating the age of sexual majority altogether* as opposed to *Arcadie's* goal of merely bringing the ages for heterosexual and homosexual acts into alignment with one another.

## The *Front homosexuel d'action révolutionnaire* (the FHAR)

> Workers of the world, caress!
> *Le Front homosexuel d'action révolutionnaire*, 1972[5]

During one of *Arcadie's* meetings in the winter of 1970, one of the women members present, Françoise d'Eaubonne, offered a simple yet fundamentally disruptive criticism to André Baudry, a comment that on its own can be understood as an initial spark for the kinds of political action that would follow: "You say that society must integrate homosexuals, but I say that homosexuals must disintegrate society!"[6] She was eventually excluded from the group, along with other women members, and together they left for the newly formed women's liberation association, the *Mouvement de libération des femmes* (or MLF). The growing presence of lesbians in the MLF, along with the nagging question of whether "one can really be a feminist and also truly love men,"[7] provided the environment necessary for issues of homosexuality to come to the forefront of the new movement, which until that point had concerned itself more with issues affecting heterosexual women, and particularly, with the issue of abortion. Gradually, an alliance, implicit at first and explicit later on, formed between members of the MLF and the increasingly dissatisfied and displaced young homosexuals of *Arcadie*. The MLF's strategies, and notably, the desire from the new members to "disintegrate" society rather than to be integrated by it, resonated particularly well for the younger members of *Arcadie*, who had begun to recognize that *Arcadie*'s strategies of dignity and respectability had produced almost no tangible changes over the many years of its serene existence.

These sentiments remained diffused, however, until March 10, 1971, a *"date fondatrice"* in the words of Eaubonne,[8] when a conference, titled "Homosexuality, this painful problem,"[9] was aired live on the radio in Paris. Ménie Grégoire, a well-known radio announcer at the French station RTL, hosted the show, whose discussants included *Arcadie*'s André Baudry, Father Guinchard,[10] Paul Mirguet (the sponsor of the 1960 law), and the future gay militant, Pierre Hahn. During the show, Pierre Hahn recognized a number of familiar women's faces in the audience as allies from the MLF. As Father Guinchard took the floor, Pierre Hahn made a sign to his friends. Françoise d'Eaubonne recounts the events that followed: "Seated in his throne next to Ménie Grégoire, Father Guinchard ... took the floor and began: 'I often hear confessions from homosexuals who come to talk to me about this painful problem ...' A beautifully resonant voice erupted from the audience: 'It's not true! We are not suffering!' "[11]

With this cry, the individuals Pierre Hahn had recognized rushed the stage, overturning chairs and microphones, screaming "declarations of war in an indescribable brouhaha."[12]

> Ménie Grégoire, in a panic, regained control of the microphone: "Something incredible is happening! Homosexuals are rushing the stage! Cut! Cut!" The technician, laughing hysterically, answered, "It's okay! I'll put on a marine song. It's appropriate!"

Radio listeners had no idea what was happening when they heard the cries of "liberty!" suddenly followed by: *Hardi les gars, vire au guindeau, Good bye, farewell ...* [the show's theme music].[13]

During this time, "one of the Amazon women had grabbed the priest by his collar and was shaking him like a fruit tree; Ménie Grégoire, screamed, 'Stop, you filthy dyke!' The girl stopped without letting go of her prey and answered with dignity: '*Madame*, that's not what I am. But upon hearing you, I have only one desire, which is to become one.' And bang, bang, the poor ecclesiastic's head on the table ..." Terrorized, Ménie Grégoire fled the scene to her dressing room, where she was seen a little while later, a glass of scotch in her hand, saying "I was not mistaken, the subject is burning hot."[14] This event served to crystallize the diffused energies and frustrations of a new generation of militants, and immediately following, the individuals who had stormed the show formed the *Front homosexuel d'action révolutionnaire* or "FHAR."[15] It is important to note that though the initial founders of the FHAR were feminists, lesbians did not remain members of the organization for long. After only a few months, the male members stopped listening to what the women had to say and began to call them "romantic schoolgirls," because they allegedly only wanted to talk about love, not sex.[16] Very early on, "misogyny reappeared with such force that the women, who were in the process of challenging the very foundations of male domination, found it intolerable."[17] By the summer of 1971, all the women had left the FHAR to form a new group called the *Gouines Rouges* (Red Dykes).

The FHAR represented a new kind of radicalism in French homosexual politics and a direct affront to *Arcadie*'s ideals of respectability and dignity. The goals of the nascent FHAR differed in several important ways from those of *Arcadie*: *Arcadie*'s more subtle tolerance of sex between adults and minors was replaced with an explicit demand for the elimination of a sexual age of majority altogether; the FHAR's strategies relied on the notion that society as a whole needed to be changed, as opposed to *Arcadie*'s hope of reforming homosexuals into "decent" citizens within the existing order; and finally, while *Arcadie* formed alliances with and gained approval from France's cultural, intellectual, economic, and political elite, the FHAR associated itself with the more radical elements of French left-wing politics and considered the overthrow of the capitalist system an integral part of its goals of sexual liberation. Despite the continued presence of discriminatory laws in France, the FHAR represented a complete change in strategies, fighting for, and to some degree achieving, an explosion of radical expressions of sexual freedom within French society.

Figures like Guy Hocquenghem and Daniel Guérin are emblematic of this exceptional time. Like many others in the FHAR, they were well educated, they saw the struggle for homosexual liberation as inextricably linked to the ideals of the political far left, and they both openly defended sexual relations with youth. Guérin had begun his political militancy with the anarchist left back in the 1930s but explained that it was in fact his sexual dissidence that was originally responsible for his political dissidence: "I came to socialism via phallism. I did not become a socialist out of pity, because of feelings of fraternity flowing from my heart, nor from reading theory... but from having early on looked for the company of young working-class guys to get off with."[18] Guérin is also known for coining his own version of the American phrase, "the personal is political," which he formulated as "our asses are revolutionary." Hocquenghem also came from the far left, having belonged to the youth section of the French Communist Party in 1962, before joining the Trotskyists in 1965, and eventually participating in the riots of May 1968. Like others in the FHAR, he had strong academic credentials, having studied philosophy at France's prestigious *Ecole normale supérieure*; and with regard to pederasty, he spoke freely and fondly of his first sexual experiences at the age of fifteen with one of his teachers.[19]

The FHAR's demand for a repeal of the age of sexual majority, framed in terms of the "liberation of young people's sexuality," was perceived as necessarily linked to the goals of revolutionary socialism. Gérard Bach-Ignasse, a gay militant from the time, recalls that in the 70s, *Arcadie's* justification of sex between adults and minors based on references to classical Greece was replaced with ideas grounded more in terms of liberation:

> In the 70s, pedophilia was a part of the global calls for more freedom. It was also a movement led by young people, so *Arcadie's* references to classical Greece made less sense. They were calling for liberation in general, without the references to classical Greece. In

the early 70s, with the FHAR, for example, "sexual relations between generations" became a central part of their platform, and they were able to couch it in terms of Leftist ideas of liberation. They talked about the age of majority in terms of age discrimination.[20]

The FHAR's journal, *Antinorm*, provided the reasoning behind the organization's defense of sex between adults and minors, arguing that sexuality begins to stir early in childhood: "Very young boys have a considerable sexual capacity, their sexuality blossoms well before the time when their genital organs are mature for reproduction... After puberty, the sexual capacity becomes surprising. The peak is somewhere between 15 and 19 years..."[21] Relying on the writings of Wilhelm Reich, the article then goes on to argue that sexual repression among children and adolescents leads to a variety of psychological disorders: "A child, thus quite early on, likes pleasure, but also very early also, repression begins.... That is when the problems of youth begin, ... feelings of guilt, neurotic worrying, disturbing sexual trouble, dissatisfaction and aggressiveness."[22] Finally, the article establishes a connection between the struggle for the "liberation of young people's sexuality" and the goals of revolutionary socialism. According to the FHAR, the goal of repressing sexual activity "is to produce an individual who fits into the authoritarian order and who will submit to it regardless of all the misery and degradation."[23] The article concludes, "socialism alone can realize sexual liberation;"[24] and when the Revolution occurs, "the youth will march in the first row of the assembly, precisely because of the great material and authoritarian oppression that has subjugated them and unites all young people to one another."[25]

Although the FHAR's overt defense of pederastic relations is the strongest indication of its radicalism compared to both older groups like *Arcadie,* and organizations appearing later on in the 1980s, other demands point in the same direction. One example is the FHAR's defense of public nudity, couched in terms of class: "nudity blurs the visible criteria of wealth based on clothing (a worker wears blue, a bourgeois man wears a suit and tie, a student has the hippie look)."[26] As a result, some of the FHAR's members conducted meetings with everyone naked.[27] Another example comes from Alain Huet's memory of Daniel Guérin: "The only thing that I heard [Guérin] fight for over and over was the end of 'ageism.' Or against the anti-older-man segregation (the older men were no longer consumable!). Or else in a more positive way, the creation of a 'sexual service' made up of youth for older men."[28]

Guy Hocquenghem and other members of the FHAR were aware of the potential power of their radicalism compared to older expressions of political militancy. Hocquenghem's book, *Le désir homosexual,* published in 1972, provided a bold articulation of that generation's belief in the possibility for total change. Hocquenghem sought to eliminate the heterosexual/homosexual binary, not through the assimilation of homosexuals, but through the recognition of the primacy and autonomy of desire and through the awareness that "the incongruent character of homosexual desire makes it dangerous for the dominant sexuality. Every day a thousand homosexual behaviors defy any classification that one tries to impose on them."[29] For Hocquenghem, it was the responsibility of homosexual movements to work toward a "sexualization of the world" and toward the abolition of the French Republic's distinction between public and private. In 1972, the FHAR in a direct response to the strategies of *Arcadie,* echoed Hocquenghem's calls for subversion when it announced "our goal is not to achieve a place in society, we are striving to disturb rather than be accepted."[30] The FHAR's strategies were based on the notion that *Arcadie*'s policies of respectability and dignity had failed and that the time had come for homosexuality to be displayed publicly and valued for its difference. Jacques Girard remembered the movement as "an abrupt eruption of free homosexual voices, which had been repressed for centuries. Three years [after the student revolts of May 1968], it was '68 for homosexuals. It arose from a decades-long guilty silence, a need to 'admit' that which will never shut itself up again."[31]

In this way, the FHAR offered a new political agenda and strategy for French homosexuals, through which French homosexuals would no longer aim for the republican goals of integration or assimilation but for an acceptance of their difference. This change of political strategy was not brought about by any changes in the laws, but rather, by way of the changing social climate emerging from the events of May '68. The anti-republican demand for tolerance of difference remained at the forefront of political action through the first half of the 70s. However, by the late 70s gay militants began to replace the demand for "the right to difference" with "the right to indifference," as French gay militants returned to a strategy of assimilation and social integration. In the early 70s, members of the FHAR considered that a return to assimilationist strategies was inevitable, as evidenced by this potentially prophetic statement:

> We must recognize... that one day we will have to fight other homosexuals who refuse to liberate themselves and prefer to integrate themselves into bourgeois society.[32]

## The *Groupes de libération homosexuelle* (the GLHs)

Internal struggles among the leaders of the FHAR eventually led to a splintering off of its members in 1974. The most significant product of this disintegration was the establishment of regional *Groupes de libération homosexuelle* (or GLHs). These new groups differed from the FHAR not only in their structure, opting for a decentralized organization of regionally based units as opposed to the FHAR's Pariscentric approach, but also in their relationship to the political far left. The new GLHs maintained the FHAR's strategy of a "right to difference" and preserved the general radicalism first enounced by the FHAR. However, the GLHs disagreed with the FHAR's conviction that French homosexuals benefited from an association with Marxist or Trotskyist politics.

Since its creation, the FHAR had sought allies with France's far left. The French left, however, remained indifferent, and sometimes even overtly hostile, to the demands of the FHAR. Many on the left continued to think of homosexuality as decadent, "bourgeois" behavior. The FHAR tried to subvert this idea by suggesting that homosexuals had a lot in common with other socially marginalized groups, and that it would be appropriate to include the struggle for homosexual liberation among other struggles for liberation. However, for many on the left, opinions of homosexuality were slow to change, and the FHAR's strategy of alliance eventually proved to be largely ineffective. For the nascent GLHs, the FHAR's strategy had been a failure and had restricted the FHAR's ability to act independently. As a consequence, the GLHs began to focus instead on building an autonomous movement for sexual liberation.

The FHAR's struggle for a "right to difference" remained central to the programs of the GLHs. Upon their creation, the GLHs were described as "an ally of all homosexuals who associate themselves with being publicly out."[33] The radicalism of the FHAR's demands, and particularly, the centrality of the issues of pederasty and pedophilia, was mirrored in the program of the new GLHs. In their *Charter of Fundamental Principles*, the GLHs provided twelve specific goals for which the organization was fighting. The fifth of these principles stated that "the GLHs fight against the idea that official sexual information should be limited to sex whose only goal is procreation, and for the idea that it take into account all forms of sexuality, beginning with children's sexuality, the very individuals to whom it is taught."[34] This is followed by the sixth principle, which states that "the blossoming of an individual in all areas including sexuality begins in childhood; this is why the GLHs fight for the recognition of a right to sexuality without any age limitation."[35] The importance of the issue of sex between adults and minors relative to other demands is evident in statements like the following: "The fight for the liberation of pederasts... is essential. This fight for liberation is essential, perhaps, more fundamental than that of homosexuals, perhaps even more than that of women. It radically questions all of society; subversion *par excellence*."[36] The centrality of the issue is further evidenced by the ways in which it spilled over to other issues, including their position on marriage and the nuclear family and on the possibility for a political alliance with feminists.

The seventh principle of the *Charter of Fundamental Principles* explicitly takes on the model of a traditional, nuclear family as well as the institution of marriage: "The GLHs do not seek equality with heterosexuals, who, also prisoners of legislation and of a way of thinking reproduced by the family..., remain incapable of living socially and sexually as free men and women."[37] Jan-Paul Pouliquen, a former GLH militant, recalls the reactions of 70s gay militants to the idea of gay marriage: "I remember a meeting when we militants talked about the possibility of what we called at the time, 'a life in common.' The conversation lasted about five minutes, because we immediately said, 'no way, that's something from the hetero-cops – it's a bourgeois thing.' And that was it. It never came up again."[38] The GLHs' antipathy toward marriage was not only linked to their position on the issue of sex between adults and minors. It was also based on the notion that the social and sexual norms associated with traditional marriages inevitably led to a restriction of individual freedom: "[In

a homosexual couple,] the roles recreate themselves, the same con-
ventions, the same compromises, the small accommodations and
the big lies. Far from constituting an original form of coupling, the
homosexual couple reproduces most often the premade schema
of marital relations. Sure, we attach less importance to fidelity, we
arrange our lives in common differently – but not much – we end up
hardly recognizing ourselves in it. Homosexual marriage, a utopia?
Homosexual couple as sexual paradise? No more than the heterosexual couple."[39] Yet at the same time, gay militants of the time recognized the inevitability of a reproduction of the model of heterosexual
couples among homosexuals, because "transgressing the social order
every day is exhausting. The homosexual couple [will continue] to
recreate a second species of normality... They are responding to the
desire to enter into the ranks, to participate like others in the fine
social order."[40]

It is important to note, however, that the GLHs' antimarriage, anti-
nuclear family stance is directly linked to their positions on pederasty and pedophilia, as witnessed by their argument that the role
of caretaker or of parent is simply a disguised form of ownership of
children, not entirely different from the dominance exerted by an
adult in a pederastic relationship:

> Here, we meddle with the domain of the children's owners – those
> who support the adoption of laws for the protection of young
> people – [a desire] that exists in every or almost every parent or
> legal guardian. Paradoxically, full of hypocrisy in fact, they make
> the following argument to fight against pederasts: "pederasts do
> not respect children, they influence them, they take possession of
> them." All I'm saying is that this is a fight between owners.[41]

This same idea was also presented during a weekend of debates on
the topic of sex between adults and minors. According to one of the
participants, "one of the most worn-out statements is the one about
the so-called 'protection of the child.' I think it is all about the monopoly of the family. The hypocrisy of it is what disgusts me the most."[42]

The issue of sex between adults and minors came to the forefront
in the GLHs' attempts to form an alliance with feminist groups.
The notion among many members of the GLHs was that women
in general, and feminists in the MLF in particular, had too strong

of a sentimental and traditional understanding of childhood to be sympathetic to the GLHs' defense of pederasty and pedophilia. Alain Huet, president of the GLHs, explained that "when you talk about pedophiles with a group of feminists, for example, some of them become hysterical anti-pederasts."[43]

From these types of statements, it is clear that the radical demands first enounced by the FHAR had for the most part survived beyond the early days of the GLHs. However, it did not take long for some members of the GLHs to begin to express a desire for a more socially acceptable political platform and for a relaxing of the radical demands that had characterized the groups' beginning. By 1976, this increasingly vocal dissent from within the GLHs, most common among the younger members, had become difficult to manage and appease. The GLHs began to divide into two factions: the first, composed primarily of older members, many of whom had begun their political activism in the FHAR, who sought to preserve the initial radicalism of the movement; and the second, made up of new, younger members, who saw the possibility for greater social acceptance and political efficacy by abandoning some of the more radical demands.

The younger members of the GLHs began to court representatives of the socialist party, who had at last become responsive to their demands. The association of some GLH members with the socialists amplified the internal tensions among the GLHs' leaders, resulting in a stalemate over a number of issues. It was out of recognition of the inefficacy of this ideological deadlock that the *Comité d'urgence anti-répression homosexuelle* was born.

The homosexual politics of the 1970s, as embodied in the FHAR and the GLHs, were of an entirely different character than that of the movements preceding them. Though they provided the framework for outbursts of expressions of freedom, they did so without successfully bringing about any corresponding legal change. Their expressions of freedom did provide a space for the movements that followed, and in particular the CUARH. However, beyond setting the stage for later, more politically effective movements, the FHAR and GLHs were of relatively weak political significance. Their rhetoric was too radical to be taken seriously by mainstream French political parties – their defense of pederastic relations was a particularly strong obstacle. The movements that followed, however, increasingly abandoned the anti-republican rhetoric of radical difference, in exchange for a more assimilationist discourse, and in so doing, were increasingly effective in eliminating the legal discriminations, and eventually in providing opportunities for social integration of French homosexuals. Groups of the late 70s recognized that real change would occur only through careful and strategic restructuring of the political demands.

## The *Comité d'urgence anti-répression homosexuelle* (the CUARH)

The *Comité d'urgence anti-répression homosexuelle* (or CUARH) was formed in July of 1979. Its former leader, Jan-Paul Pouliquen, recalls the ways in which the CUARH represented a new form of gay politics:

> Homosexuals and their groups were not recognized by anyone, including the political parties on the left... I figured that in order to finally be recognized a little bit, ... we had to make the homosexual movement acceptable to the parties and unions... When we had the first meeting with the Ministers, I wore a suit, and those who had pink hair with feathers in it, well, I told them that they couldn't come to the meeting... And I don't regret acting like that now twenty years later. I said we are there to work, not to act like idiots.[44]

The main goal of the CUARH was to serve as a new professionalized political force for French homosexuals, by serving as an umbrella organization with the aim of rising above the internal struggles plaguing the movement. Its hope was to offer a single voice for the various splintered groups of the time, with the idea that internal struggles could be dealt with elsewhere, that despite the differences of opinion among various political leaders, French homosexuals shared at least some common goals, and most notably the repeals of discriminatory laws. It succeeded in bringing together representatives from other homosexual movements, including the *Groupes de libération homosexuelle* (the GLHs), the *Comités homosexuels d'arrondissement*, *David et Jonathan* (a Christian homosexual group), *Beit Havérim* (a Jewish homosexual group) and the *Centre du Christ libérateur du Pasteur Doucé*.

Rapidly, the CUARH succeeded in monopolizing the political power of French homosexuals, quickly becoming the "lance of homosexual militancy in France."[45] Its first political action consisted of a violent reaction against the senate's decision to align its position with the national assembly's support for the 1942 law. The CUARH published a call to action, where it declared that the senate had "thus ceded to the will of all those who are developing an anti-homosexual racism today. At a time when the entire country has risen up against the upsurge of racism, the Senate comes and gives a line of reasoning to fascist groups, who, like the *Renouveau français*, are signing today a petition demanding that 'the application of Article 331 [i.e., the 1942 law] be solidly maintained and that all foreign homosexuals be expelled.'"[46] Among the hundreds of signatures are the names of some of the most important homosexual militants and public intellectuals sympathetic to the homosexual cause of the time: Louis Aragon, Gisèle Halimi, Georges Kiejman, Alain Krivine, Costa Gavras. Shortly after this, the CUARH organized a protest for October 23, 1980, which succeeded in bringing together two thousand people.[47]

The question of the age of sexual majority continued to occupy a place among the political issues of concern to the CUARH. Among members of the CUARH, a debate continued over the position the CUARH should take with regard to the 1942 law: should the organization call for the elimination of the age of sexual majority altogether or should the demand be that the ages for homosexuals and heterosexuals be the same? While the majority of members were increasingly leaning toward the latter option, one of the CUARH's most engaged and vocal militants, Gérard Bach-Ignasse, defended the former:

> The homosexual movement can content itself with asking for the end of discrimination against homosexuals, or it can go further by calling into question laws that restrict any sexual act, gay or straight, for individuals under fifteen years of age. Homosexuals who are looking for a rapid integration into society are especially averse to the question of pederasty, which is too troublesome in their eyes. But if we think about it, the question of pederasty and of childhood sexuality is today the core of sexual liberation, including homosexual liberation.[48]

The fact that Bach-Ignasse could maintain this position within the CUARH is indicative of the organization's capacity to accommodate conflicting points of view. While the CUARH presented itself publicly with a single, moderated voice, its success was also linked to its ability to provide a forum for internal debate. In the end, what distinguished the CUARH from the earlier movements of the 1970s was its ability to be heard by leaders of the socialist party and by French society at large. The CUARH made "no bones about its 'pragmatic approach' [by] fostering contacts with the press, trade unions and political parties and lobbying them for an end to discrimination."[49] Its public voice was moderate and its prevailing public strategy was assimilationist. The association was politically successful not only because it presented itself as the single voice for all French homosexuals, but also because it successfully distanced its own representations of homosexuality from the representations of homosexuality made earlier in the decade by the FHAR and the GLHs. The CUARH managed to represent itself *publicly* as a moderate political movement by keeping radical and dissenting voices appeased through *private,* internal discussion forums. The successful repeal of the discriminatory laws that followed can be attributed to various causes, and in particular, the victory of the socialists in the elections of 1981. However, the professionalized lobbying of the CUARH and its reliance on assimilationist principles prior to the 1981 elections was certainly a necessary, albeit perhaps insufficient, causal antecedent for the eventual repeals.

### The repeal of the 1960 law

French legislators had less difficulty repealing the 1960 public indecency law than the 1942 law concerning the age of sexual majority. A look at the parliamentary debates demonstrates that concerns over pederasty and pedophilia and their association with male homosexuality were the primary obstacle to the 1942 law's repeal – an indication that the radicalism of the movements from the early 70s might even be held partly responsible for making the repeal of the 1942 law more difficult. The earlier groups had served to strengthen the association of male homosexuality with pederasty and pedophilia, effectively creating paranoia among lawmakers who thought that to repeal the 1942 law would create a slippery slope that would bring about a greater acceptance of sex between adults and minors, and eventually, the elimination of the age of sexual majority altogether. It is important to note that the repeal of the 1960 law took place at a time prior to the CUARH's articulation of more moderate demands, while for the 1942 law, it was necessary first for the CUARH to silence any public defense of pederasty and pedophilia before the socialists would be willing to listen them.

The history of the repeal of the 1960 law begins on December 21, 1977, when President Giscard d'Estaing called for a commission to revise the penal code directed by Senator Henri Caillavet. Caillavet's goal of "rationalizing" the penal code led him to bring a bill "seeking the suppression of any discrimination against homosexuals, and more precisely, the elimination of Paragraph 2 of Article 330 [the 1960 law] and of Paragraph 3 of Article 331 [the 1942 law]."[50] The discussion of Caillavet's bill took place the following spring, in 1978, at the time of the Commission's discussion of the revision of the penal code, including several propositions concerning the repression of rape, and on June 28, 1978, the senate adopted Caillavet's proposition for the repeal of both laws.

Between June 1978 and November 1980, however, the bill would go back and forth many times between the senate and the national assembly; and in the process, it became increasingly clear that both laws could not be repealed at the same time.[51] On December 23, 1980, a bill was at last adopted that repealed the 1960 law but left the 1942 law in the new penal code. French homosexuals would have to wait for the arrival of the Socialists in 1981 and the lobbying efforts of the CUARH to witness its repeal. During the numerous back-and-forth movements of the bill, there were relatively few debates over the 1960 law, compared to the number over the 1942 law. Yet given that the same principles of equality and nondiscrimination would appear to justify the repeal of both, why did the issue of the age of sexual majority give rise to so many more noisy disputes than the question of public indecency? How could the senators and deputies have justified the elimination of discrimination in only one of the two cases?

Among those who voted for the repeal of the 1960 law, but defended the 1942 law, the Minister of the Family, Monique Pelletier, was particularly vocal, and provided an explanation for treating the two cases differently: "The main concern is the protection of adolescents...Are they not fragile and vulnerable? We also believe then that a decriminalization could be seen by certain individuals as incitement."[52] When she says "vulnerable," to what danger was the adolescent in her mind actually susceptible? Was she implying here that homosexuality is a particular taste that one might acquire at a young age through homosexual experiences, but that after a certain age, the danger of becoming homosexual disappears? Jean-Paul Mourot, a junior minister in the government at the time, echoed Pelletier's line of reasoning, by saying that the repeal of the 1942 law "would be seen, or risked being seen, as an encouragement for adult homosexuals to seduce adolescents under eighteen...The Government has rallied behind this concern for prevention, and I insist strongly on the term 'prevention.'"[53] One problem with the defenses of the 1942 law made by Pelletier and Mourot is that they present no justification for a stronger repression of homosexual relations between adults and adolescents than for heterosexual relations between adults and adolescents, since their statements regarding the "protection of adolescents" could apply equally to both. The only way to justify a stronger repression of homosexual acts would be to claim that homosexual relations with minors are more dangerous or somehow qualitatively worse than heterosexual relations with minors, which neither Mourot nor Pelletier do explicitly in their defenses of the 1942 law.

At least two types of arguments might be used to justify the idea that homosexual relations with minors are more harmful than heterosexual relations with minors. The first would be the allegation that homosexuals are more inclined to have sexual relations with minors than heterosexuals are. The second would be the claim that any homosexual activity is harmful both to the individuals practicing the acts and perhaps to society at large, and that a first step toward eliminating homosexuality altogether would be to put an end to the supposed vector for homosexual contagion: from sexual contacts between adults and minors of the same sex. This line of reasoning could be further substantiated if one assumes that the possibility for homosexual contagion is significantly higher when one is young, and that after a certain age the risk of becoming homosexual begins to decrease.

The first of these lines of reasoning regarding the dangers of homosexuality relies on assumptions about the frequency of homosexual relations between adults and minors, while the second depends on the specific qualitative nature of these acts. But even if the frequency of sexual acts between adults and minors were higher among homosexuals than heterosexuals (a notion that has been disproved[54]), the stronger repression of homosexual relations with minors might be considered socially desirable, without making it juridically justifiable. Basic principles of equality do not allow for a greater frequency of criminality within a specific segment of the population to be grounds for a different law aimed specifically at that group. For example, even if it is true that the number of murders committed by men each year exceeds the number committed by women, the law establishing the crime of murder cannot punish men more harshly than women for the same act.

However, it is acceptable to distinguish among various groups when there is a qualitative difference. Thus, if one accepts the second line of reasoning according to which homosexual relations with minors are by their nature harmful because any homosexual relation is harmful, then it would make sense to attack more harshly the vector by which homosexuality is allegedly most effectively transmitted. At least legally speaking, this kind of reasoning makes it easier to justify a distinction between heterosexual and homosexual relations. This is why in reference to the 1942 law, the Constitutional Council declared in 1980 that the principle of equality "does not present an obstacle to any differentiation operated under penal law between actions of *different nature,*" and that the law may "without any misinterpretation of the principle of equality, distinguish in the interest of the protection of minors, between acts committed between persons of the same sex and those committed between persons of different sexes."[55]

The implicit message of the council and of the legislators who defended this position is that homosexuality by its very nature is necessarily harmful – even among consenting adults – otherwise, the ideas of contagion and of protection would lose their meaning. It is not hard then to imagine that those who defended the law would have been happy to restrict homosexuality more broadly. So what prevented the senators from affirming explicitly in their debates that homosexuality in general represented a danger to society? Once again it seems that they were aware of the impossibility of such a feat, given the restraints of the republican legal system.

### The repeal of the 1942 law

The late 70s brought attention to the issue of sexual majority, and calls for more lenient treatment of sexual relations between adults and minors came not only from radical homosexual movements, but also from members of France's literary and cultural elite. In January 1977, a letter appeared in the newspaper *Libération* calling for the release of three men who had been accused of sexual assault of boys and girls aged 13 and 14. The letter acknowledged that the men had sex with the minors, but claimed nonetheless that "the children had not been victims of the slightest violence...There is an obvious disproportionate discrepancy between the term 'crime,' which would justify such severity, and the facts of this case." It adds that "French law contradicts itself by recognizing a capacity for discernment in thirteen- and fourteen-year olds, which allows them to be tried and punished, yet denies them the same capacity when their emotional and sexual lives are concerned." The long list of signatures includes Louis Aragon, Roland Barthes, Gilles Deleuze, Françoise d'Eaubonne, Jean-Paul Sartre, Simone de Beauvoir, Philippe Sollers, and Jack Lang.[56] Later that same year, the commission for the revision of the penal code received a petition demanding that the code eliminate any reference to the age of sexual majority altogether. Among those who signed the petition were Louis Althusser, Jacques Derrida, André Glucksmann, Guy Hocquenghem, and Michel Foucault.[57] The legislators heard these calls, although they certainly did not produce the desired effect. If anything they only added to the difficulty and the delay associated with repealing the 1942 law.

The association of male homosexuality with pederasty and pedophilia influenced the legal debates and was the main reason why the 1960 law was repealed more easily than the 1942 law, which survived until August 4, 1982.[58] During the senate's first reading of the bill on May 4, 1982, Senator Etienne Dailly put forth rather explicitly the association of male homosexuality with pederasty and pedophilia in a long defense of the 1942 law, which remarkably through its reliance on notions of contagion, resembled quite strongly the kinds of testimonies made by medical experts a century earlier.[59] First he established that homosexuality is not inborn: "The innateness of homosexuality in the sense of a somatic, genetic, original substratum cannot be defended."[60] Dailly then defended the notion that there is a time in life when one is particularly vulnerable to homosexual desires, which if acted upon, can fix an individual's sexual orientation as homosexual for the rest of his or her life. He presented a study that concluded that "homosexuality is not an innate phenomenon,

but a behavior that is acquired: it is not however necessarily perman-
ent and can be the result of continued experience; it is thus appropriate, not to allow [such experiences] to occur among the youth,
who are particularly vulnerable; insofar as his/her sexual tendencies
have not yet been permanently determined."[61] In the last part of his
discussion, Dailly went on to explain how these ideas are relevant to
the question of the repeals:

> Adolescence – and who would dare claim that one is done with
> it before the age of 18? – must be particularly protected from
> homosexual assaults. If one holds that it is perfectly admissible to
> have removed any discrimination against adult homosexuality, it
> nonetheless remains absolutely necessary to protect individuals
> from homosexual acts during the time in their lives when they
> are most fragile and when they might be easy prey for those who
> practice homosexuality.[62]

In his speech, the importance granted to the republican legal system's requirement that every crime must have a victim is apparent.
Dailly, through his implicit references to contagion, was trying to
convince his audience that the 1942 law did indeed have an identifiable victim.

During the second reading by the senate, Gisèle Halimi, representing the commission on constitutional law, reacted to Dailly's speech.
Her response is a classic example of republican rhetoric inspired by
the values of secularism and liberalism: "Sexual morality must be
considered as having the same characteristics as religious morality
or 'a-religious' morality: it must be seen as arising from personal
choice and individual conscience." She then upheld the republican
notion that the state cannot restrict an individual's freedom "unless
there is violence or harm done...I am surprised that the eminent
legal scholars who oppose the repeal have not been sensitive to
the legal necessity to do away with such a law."[63] The same debates
continued between Halimi and Dailly until July, when during its
fourth reading, the national assembly finally adopted the text. "He
is fifteen years old, he is free!" declared the magazine *Gai pied* in
September 1982, adding that the reform "radically alters the freedom
available for transgressive fantasy from before the repeal, it shakes
up our overly idealistic belief in the 'myth of lost adolescence,' and

finally, it sets up in bold letters a new symbolic frontier for adult-child relations."[64]

The history of gay political movements in the 1970s shows how the most radical calls for freedom as articulated in the early part of the decade did not coincide with changes in the laws affecting homosexuals. Legal change did not occur until the anti-republican calls for a "right to difference" in the early 70s were abandoned in exchange for a universalist, republican discourse of sameness. It is difficult in this context to ascertain the exact nature of the bidirectional causal relationship between social movements and the law. On the one hand, with regard to how the law shaped social movements in the early 70s, the presence of discriminatory laws did little to limit the freedom of French homosexuals, even if the subject matter of these laws (public sex and pederasty) did shape the character of the movements' demands. On the other hand, with regard to how social movements influenced legal change, it is important to see how the anti-republican articulations of radical difference in the early 70s produced little tangible benefits and in fact, may have even served to delay the legal repeals – an indication of the republic's resiliency and its ability to resist subversion. It was only through the more moderate demands of the CUARH that the most difficult legal reform was able to occur in the form of repeal of the 1942 law.

These same issues will remain relevant in the 1980s, a time when French law ceased making any distinction whatsoever between heterosexual and homosexual acts. Somewhat paradoxically, this new era of legal tolerance was also a time when French homosexuals began to censor more and more the representations they made of themselves, avoiding for example, associations with the less socially palatable elements of early 70s homosexual movements. This new generation of French homosexuals sought to present itself as essentially the same as other French people; to move away from anti-republican notions of difference and toward ever greater social integration. By the mid-70s, some homosexual activists could already see this change coming – the following prophetic statement from the GLHs' journal *Sexpol* in 1976 indicates their awareness of the inevitability of a shift in political strategy: "Homosexuality will need to become bourgeois in order to be accepted."[65]

# 3
# French Homosexuals Build a more Stately Closet (The 1980s–2000s)[1]

> Build thee more stately mansions, O my soul,
> As the swift seasons roll!
> Leave thy low-vaulted past!
> Let each new temple, nobler than the last,
> Shut thee from heaven with a dome more vast,
> Till thou at length art free,
> Leaving thine outgrown shell by life's unresting sea!
>                 "The Chambered Nautilus" Oliver Wendell Holmes[2]

In their founding myths most contemporary gay organizations in France have sought to portray themselves as heirs of the revolutionary ideas introduced by the gay political groups that were formed in the early 70s. However, this teleological interpretation is misleading in at least two respects. It does not recognize the magnitude of the disruption to French gay organizations that occurred in the late 70s and early 80s, and it fails to account for the ethos of assimilation that now prevails in many of France's active gay groups. Immediately following the repeal of the 1960 law and the 1942 law, the political and cultural arenas of French homosexuality changed markedly. As the timeline (Figure 3.1) indicates, virtually all of the then extant French gay cultural and political organizations were abruptly dissolved and new groups were formed.[3] Moreover, as representations of homosexuals fell into alignment with the French Republic's longstanding requirements for assimilation and acceptance, the legal and public constraints of the earlier period were replaced with internalized, private, self-controls.

In place of the prevailing myth noted above, I would like to propose a more nuanced and more accurate, albeit decidedly less fashionable

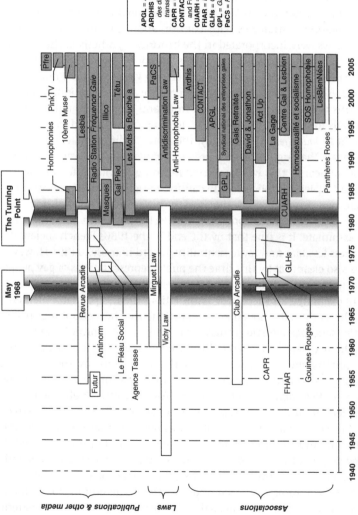

*Figure 3.1* Timeline of homosexual political movements, laws, and media in France (1942–2008)

Key to Acronyms

**APGL** = Association des parents gays et lesbiens
**ARDHIS** = Association pour la reconnaissance des droits des personnes homosexuelles et transsexuelles à l'immigration et au séjour
**CAPR** = Comité d'action pédérastique révolutionnaire
**CONTACT** = French version of PFLAG (Parents, Families, and Friends of Lesbians and Gays)
**CUARH** =Comité d'urgence anti-répression homosexuelle
**FHAR** = Front homosexuel d'action révolutionnaire
**GLHs** = Groupes de libération homosexuelle
**GPL** = Gais pour la liberté
**PaCS** = Pacte civil de solidarité

and less politically appealing, interpretation of recent French gay political history. It is one of thesis, antithesis, and synthesis. For nearly two decades after its founding in the mid-1950s, the dominant political and social organization for French homosexuals was Club Arcadie whose aim was to present homosexuals as respectable, cultured, and dignified individuals deserving of greater social tolerance. In the early 1970s this thesis of homosexual respectability was challenged by an antithesis, when the FHAR and the GLHs, sought to replace republican assimilationist strategies with confrontation. In turn, these competing views were incorporated in the historical synthesis of the new gay political and cultural communities founded in the 1980s. After the repeals of legislation noted earlier, French gays seized the new opportunities to gain increased social acceptance and integration. Indicative of this is the shift that occurred from anti-republican, antiuniversalist calls for a "right to difference" to a discourse framed in terms of a "right to *indifference*." Generally, the word "indifferent" is understood to mean "having no bias, or preference; neutral."[4] However, it is possible to hear in this word a second meaning of "not different" or "the same." At least implicit in the call for a "right to indifference," then, were two demands: first, that society have no bias toward homosexuals; and second, that homosexuals have the possibility to be the same, to assimilate. It is true that by the end of the 1980s French society did express less bias and more neutrality toward homosexuality. However, it is also clear that by this time the public representations of gay people had become less different, that is, more indifferent.

In exchange for successful assimilation, the less palatable elements of the early '70s movements – particularly the pedophilic, pederastic, sadomasochistic, transsexual, transvestite, promiscuous, and public-sex elements – had to be excluded or at least ignored by those occupying the new gay spaces of the '80s. Thus, by the mid-'80s, through a process of exclusion within the gay community itself, the more radical demands of the early '70s were effectively silenced, if not left behind.[5] After years of legal censure, French homosexuals had learned that external control was possible, that it would remain a threat, and that to escape future censure and to preserve society's new degree of tolerance, they had to replace external controls with self-control. It is this shift from external legal censure to an ongoing process of auto-censure that underlies the discussion in this chapter, a process of invisible, internalized control made more transparent by Michel Foucault's metaphor of the panopticon (a prison designed by the utilitarian philosopher, Jeremy Bentham, with cells arranged around a central tower from which a guard can see all the prisoners, but which does not allow prisoners to know when they are being observed, causing prisoners over time to begin to monitor their own conduct). Through the metaphor of the panopticon,

> Foucault offers another perspective on how power operates. He rejects the simple, hierarchical approach and suggests instead that power is not a unitary concept, not an absolute. Instead he says that "Power comes from below; that is, there is no binary and all-encompassing opposition between rulers and ruled at the root of power relations, and serving as a general matrix – no such duality extending from the top down and reacting on more and more limited groups to the very depths of the social body." Instead, he sees power as being dispersed through the network of relationships which make up society and based in discourse. This is not to deny that power struggle might be unequal but to suggest that it is not exercised in a single, downward vector.[6]

Foucault's panopticon model of social control is particularly apt in the context of the 1980s, a time when control was no longer exerted "downward" through legal restrictions, but through the subjects of control themselves, through their own interiorized knowledge of what was acceptable. In the 1980s, like the chambered nautilus in the Oliver Wendell Holmes's poem that introduced this chapter, French gay people created a new space for themselves, a space that in many ways was better than the one from which they had emerged. Opportunities for social assimilation increased, and gay political groups successfully lobbied for an antidiscrimination law in 1985 and for legally recognized partnerships for same-sex couples in 1999. What follows is an examination of the shifts in the construction of French homosexual identity during the 1980s and 90s in three interrelated spaces: the geographic space of the Marais; the cultural space of the gay publication *Gai pied*, and the legal-political space, beginning with the period of widespread political apathy and the excruciatingly slow response to AIDS in the early 80s, followed by a period of more pragmatic politics leading to the passage of an antidiscrimination law in 1985 and a law for civil unions available to same-sex couples in 1999. It is important to remember, however, that these geographic, cultural, and legal-political spaces are deeply interrelated and not as distinct as the separate discussions that follow might suggest.

## The neighborhood of the Marais

In the early 1980s the Marais, a small district in Paris located between the Pompidou Center and the Bastille, underwent a thorough transformation. During that time, this affluent area in the oldest part of Paris was gradually converted into France's answer to the American-style "gay ghetto" – albeit a reluctant ghetto by U.S. standards.[7] This transformed Marais provided a space for the development of a new identity, a "gay identity," for French homosexuals. As the community grew, "gay" became synonymous with "respectable," with "socially assimilable," and as the 70s gay activist Jean Le Bitoux points out, with "affluent."

After cleaning itself up, the Marais of the 1980s was finally ready to welcome a new kind of population, or perhaps, a new kind of "clientele"–one which would have not only more dynamism but also more spending power. The gay flag did not appear in individual apartment windows on the first Lesbian and Gay Pride Day, but, instead, in the windows of stores, and it stayed there for the rest of the year. Visibility or obscenity? Identity or commercial exploitation?[8]

The story of a French gay community grounded in the Marais begins in 1978 with the opening of a new bar, Le Village, in the heart of the district. Le Village presented itself as an alternative to the nocturnal homosexual life that occurred on the rue Sainte-Anne, in the shadows of the Opera Garnier. Le Village symbolized a new kind of visibility: open both day and night and offering beer for the meager sum of ten francs, the bar attracted large crowds at once. Over the next decade, waves of entrepreneurs followed, investing not only in bars, but in restaurants, boutiques, inns, and so on. Michael Sibalis offers several reasons for the shift from the rue Sainte-Anne to the Marais, including the ease with which the neighborhood can be accessed via public transportation, the aesthetic appeal of a district whose "attractiveness increased in the 1970s and 1980s, when the Marais was turned into an important cultural and artistic quarter," and finally the fact that "gay businessmen recognised that the Marais, with its low rents and real-estate prices, was ripe for investment."[9]

The result has been the transformation not only of a neighborhood, but of Parisian gay life in general. Now, more than 20 years later, the opening of Le Village has a mythic significance: it fostered a post-Stonewall gay identity in France. Proclaimed the first issue of *La revue h*:

> From Le Village to the Duplex, from the Piano Zinc to Le Central, the gay quarter set itself up in the 1980s. ... Today, we have attained a new level with boutiques, nightclubs, a bookstore, postcard shops, sex shops, restaurants, bars, clothing stores (as well as laundromats), and recently a pharmacy waving the gay flag which was inaugurated by "the entire community." Paris could at last have the honor of joining the other modern capitalist capitals with its gay neighborhood.[10]

This transformed Marais provided a space for the development of gay identities that had not existed before in France. As the community grew, French gays gained a reputation as respectable, resourceful, and socially palatable. The rainbow flag began to appear in store windows – a symptom of commercialization, certainly, but also of a new kind of visibility. As Michaël Pollak remarked at the time, "Homosexuality has come out of the shadow and from the domain of the not-talked-about."[11]

In 1981 Paris held its first Lesbian and Gay Pride parade in the Marais. This event had a double significance: it was a victory in the fight for visibility, but it was also a symptom of the growing normalization of the movement.[12] However, as one critic of these developments observed:

> It was this "happy" event which accompanied the collapse of the gay and lesbian movement, due to a sudden lack of political demands: the *minitel* [a terminal with screen connected to the telephone that could be used for online chat], the neighborhood of the Marais, the Americanization of looks and lifestyles began to take over, neglecting those who did not fit in or who were outside

of this nocturnal effervescence. Gay Pride was nothing more than a commercial carnival.[13]

The emerging community in the Marais, which may initially have been defined by a sexual orientation, became increasingly united by shared tastes, cultural preferences in music and food, and even by a distinct "Marais look" among the gay male inhabitants, who have been described as "handsome, young, muscular, white, appropriately tanned and/or shaved body with skin-tight clothing... without which, the penalty was a gaze that could kill."[14] For Foucault, it is of course the gaze, in its most general sense, that is the vector through which power is exerted in society: "There is no need for arms, physical violence, material constraints. Just a gaze. An inspecting gaze, a gaze which each individual under its weight will end by interiorisation to the point that he is his own overseer, each individual thus exercising this surveillance over, and against, himself. A superb formula: power exercised continuously and for what turns out to be minimal cost."[15]

In the new Marais, acceptability was determined not only by the gaze of its residents, but by the more general gaze of French society (and its marketing teams). At last the rest of France was interested in accepting the new, fresh, respectable consumers of the gay community – and why would it not be? The gaze of the transformed Marais assured that upon entering the neighborhood, one left behind any residual radicalism of the early '70s (including desires for perverse sex practices and residual Trotskyist leanings). In this way, the gaze of the Marais itself prevented the resulting community from posing any serious threat to the status quo.

With hindsight it is now clear that the establishment of a gay space in the Marais was inseparable from the emergence of a new kind of visibility and respectability for gays in other spaces. As the sociologist Frédéric Martel explained,

In the 1980s, a veritable gay "citizen" was born. He lived in Paris, ate his breakfast while listening to [the gay radio station] *Fréquence gaie*, worked in a gay establishment (there were over a hundred of them in Paris already), and informed himself by reading *Gai pied* .... In the evening, he would have dinner in a restaurant in the Marais and then dance until dawn at the Palace or the Broad... [It was] the beginning of the era of the body, a cultish narcissistic wave, which continued to develop through countless gyms and saunas. The new gay had arrived with string bikini and leather jacket. The queen and the sissy were gone.[16]

## The magazine *Gai pied* and the new gay imagery

In June 1982, shortly after the laws that distinguished homosexual from heterosexual conduct were repealed, Club Arcadie, the longest surviving homosexual association, was dissolved, and its magazine, *Revue Arcadie*, ceased publication. From the late 1950s until the early '70s, *Arcadie* had "been the monopoly of militant homosexuality, or more precisely, of militant 'homophilia,' since this was term the magazine had always preferred.... Until 1971, no other movement disputed the star-status of Arcadie. It was not until after May 1968 that the Arcadie's monopoly would be broken [with the arrival of groups like the FHAR and the GLHs]."[17] Throughout the '70s, *Arcadie's* membership declined, and its strategy of respectability and dignity became subject to ever harsher criticism. The dominant strategy of the newer gay movements, which involved asserting difference and working toward changing society rather changing oneself, conflicted directly with *Arcadie's* approach of presenting homosexuals as socially acceptable.

Despite its diminished importance, the end of both Club Arcadie and its magazine in 1982 was a significant event for French homosexuals, spawning a number of articles in the new magazine *Gai pied*. The general consensus, as evidenced by the articles in these magazines, was that *Arcadie* had served a purpose during the repressive decades of the '50s and '60s, but that as times changed, *Arcadie* had stubbornly refused to evolve with them, and that *Arcadie's* policy of "respectability" and "dignity" had proved to be entirely incapable of producing social change. In a letter dated May 15, 1982, the editors of *Revue Arcadie* explained their policy and their reasons for ceasing publication:

> Times have changed, far too much some would say.... This world of permissiveness, of irresponsibility, of frivolity, of obscenity – and the homophile people beat the records in this sad domain – breaks down our energies and makes the continuation of activities, which no longer correspond to those of the club's founders, entirely futile.[18]

Just prior to writing this letter, the leader of Club Arcadie, André Baudry, had been asked what he thought of the new magazine *Gai pied* and the new radio station *Fréquence gaie*:

> What I hold against *Gai pied* is its excessive advertising... As for radio... they are trying to please a certain, very limited audience of homosexuals, rowdies, eccentrics; an audience of frivolous, superficial and shallow individuals.

Baudry's view of the French gay situation in the early '80s was, of course, an easy target for ridicule, yet his observations about rising consumerism and frivolity may not have been so far off the mark. After the legal victories, it seems that French homosexuals abandoned political causes *en masse* and became more noted for their consumption of gay merchandise and services in the Marais than for political action. Like Baudry, other critics of the new generation of French homosexuals saw them as opportunists. They had benefited from the hard work of their elders, but were incapable of understanding that Club Arcadie's strategy of respectability was probably necessary, given the difficult environment of the 1950s and '60s. A kinder interpretation of the new generation in the '80s might have pointed to other factors: the absence of political leaders to mobilize political engagement, the growing opportunities for gay consumerism in the Marais, and the general sentiment that all political demands had been met, that there was nothing left to fight against, and that it was time, at last, to have fun, to be gay. A writer in *Gai pied* remembered Baudry's contribution this way:

> Baudry hasn't gone out enough and has read too much heterosexual press. If anything, modifications to the homosexual condition these last few years in France have entirely removed the guilt associated with "our problem," which Arcadie buried under tons of auto-repression and paternalistic threats.[19]

By the time *Arcadie* closed down, its meaning in the history of French homosexuality had been settled: the club and its journal had served a purpose, but changes in society's opinions of homosexuality no longer required such a "closeted" approach. What is implicit here, of course, is the idea that *Gai pied* was quite different from *Revue*

*Arcadie*: it was a magazine for the new generation of French gays; it opposed restrictions on personal freedom; it was a projection of '70s ideals. What is masked in this account are the ways in which the new magazine resembled *Revue Arcadie*: it too was promoting respectability for French gays.

There were in fact three different incarnations of the magazine *Gai pied*. The first version under the leadership of Jean Le Bitoux, a political activist from the 70s, was a "monthly magazine for information and reflection" that did not hide its political engagement and demanded "to be heard by public authorities."[20] In 1982, however, tensions began to rise among members of the editorial staff. At issue was the best way to resolve the financial difficulties the magazine was facing. Le Bitoux, who was initially reluctant to approve radical changes to the magazine he had founded, eventually accepted to change from a monthly to a weekly publication, to change the name of the magazine to *Gai pied hebdo* and to increase the amount of space devoted to advertising. He later came to regret his decision and in July 1983, a group of approximately thirty of *Gai pied*'s original writers and editors resigned. Le Bitoux explains what motivated them to do so:

> With the change to a weekly in the fall of 1982, gay advertising had invaded everything: the cover, advertising that looked like articles, product reviews that were connected to advertising, fake classified ads, etc. ... Fashion pages came after erotic confessions. Colonialist-style reports told us about inexpensive boys under the sun. ... *Gai pied [hebdo]* was nothing more than a big department store, its shelves filled with the exact opposite of the founding texts of the homosexual movement.[21]

This second incarnation of *Gai pied* lasted nearly ten years. However, the magazine, which had been financially successful for the first few years, started to lose readership at a rate of about 10 percent per year beginning in 1985, with a drop of 30 percent in 1987, the year in which French versions of American pornographic magazines began to arrive in French kiosks.[22] By the early 90s, the magazine's readership had dwindled to 9,000, which is scarcely enough to keep a magazine alive. In March 1992, the editorial staff decided to make a second radical change to the magazine's content. Rather than trying to compete with the growing number of erotic titles, this third incarnation of *Gai pied hebdo* would stop devoting any of its space to sex and redirect the magazine's focus toward politics. The decision turned out to be disastrous for sales and in October of the same year, the magazine published its last issue.

Table 3.1 shows the primary shifts in content from one period of the magazine's history to the next: from the first to the second, the amount of political news dropped precipitously, articles related to shopping began to occupy a significant number of pages, and the space devoted to sex and erotica increased; for the third version, all of the space that had been used for sex and erotica became dedicated to political news, while the allocation of space to other categories remained fairly stable.

The creation of *Gai pied hebdo* in 1982 foretold the arrival of a new cultural climate. Its articles portrayed homosexuality differently from the provocative 70s' magazines like *Antinorm* or *Le Fléau social*, offering images of stable gay couples whose sex took place in a bedroom, hardworking folks who presented no threat to the status quo. In short, gay partners were suddenly represented in the same way as any other bourgeois French couple. Conspicuously absent from this second incarnation were articles and images related to pedophilia, pederasty, transsexuals and transvestites, sadomasochism, and public sex – subjects which had appeared frequently in the press of the early '70s, but also in the first incarnation of *Gai pied* under Le Bitoux's direction. Instead, articles began to focus on such issues as adoption by gay couples, coming-out in the workplace, legal and property issues specific to gay couples, reviews of new restaurants and bars, vacation ideas, fashion trends, and other opportunities for spending "gay money." These are all topics that would have been considered too "bourgeois" by the standards of magazines like *Antinorm* and *Le Fléau social* from the early '70s. Models of French sexual outlaws, including Jean Genet, Guy Hocquenghem, and Michel Foucault, were replaced with the model of the "good" sexual citizen, and readers of *Gai pied hebdo* began to understand that a sexual second-class citizen could "move into the realm of the 'good citizen' by way of becoming a 'good consumer'."[23]

Despite the changes in *Gai pied*'s content, however, the editorial team continued to represent itself as an extension of 1970s political militancy, even if that required a bit of revisionism for potentially

Table 3.1  Allocation of space in *Gai pied* (1979–1992)[a]

| | Sex & erotica % | Political news % | Other news % | Personal ads % | Entertainment & Leisure % | Shopping % |
|---|---|---|---|---|---|---|
| **Period 1:** *Gai pied* (1979–1982) | 7.3 | 8.8 | 51.1 | 13.1 | 19.3 | 0.4 |
| **Period 2:** *Gai pied hebdo* (1982–Mar. 1992) | 14.9 | 2.3 | 44.5 | 9.6 | 22.8 | 5.9 |
| **Period 3:** *Gai pied hebdo* (Mar.–Oct. 1992) | 0.0 | 12.8 | 46.8 | 11.4 | 23.4 | 5.6 |

*Note:* [a]These data come from a sampling of 4 issues of *Gai pied*, 4 issues of *Gai pied hebdo*, and 3 issues of the new *Gai pied hebdo* that began in 1992. I developed 52 categories for articles. For each issue, I calculated the number of 1/12ths of a page devoted to each of these categories. Of the 52 categories, 3 were associated with "political news", 20 with "other news," 1 with "Personal Ads," 14 with "Entertainment / Leisure," 8 with "Shopping," and 6 with "Sex/Erotica."

pesky details. Jean Le Bitoux recalls that "[b]eginning in 1984, the editorial team who stayed on at *Gai pied [hebdo]* happily recalled its glorious past in their columns, but censorship had taken over. They avoided citing the names of some of the founding members or of those who quit."[24]

In the new gay imagery of the 1980s, glossy pictures of handsome men began to appear with greater frequency. Unlike the images of waiflike adolescents that dominated the revues of the early '70s, with their pederastic implications, the prevailing images of the '80s were quite clearly of adults – men with fully formed, strong bodies and abundant facial hair. This provoked one anonymous contributor to *Gai pied hebdo* to ask whether the appreciation of "clean, adult, and healthy homosexuals did not lead at the same time to a reinforcement of the repression of pedophiles."[25] One observer described this visual transformation as follows:

> With the arrival of the Village People and Helmut Berger's photos, a new virile aesthetic dominated. Omnipresent in the first Brentwood erotic films or in Tom of Finland's legendary comic strips and its beefcakes, the aesthetic invaded personal ads.... You had to be muscular, virile and especially, young. These examples illustrate the profound mutation in gay imagery of the last 30 years.[26]

In the early '80s, the French writer and former FHAR militant Guy Hocquenghem expressed his dissatisfaction with the image of the new gay man:

> The classic queens (both the friendly and malicious ones); those who appreciated trouble-makers; the tearoom specialists and all those who could trace their colorful ways back to the 19th century are disappearing before the comforting modernity of the 25- to 40-year-old mustached homosexual with his attaché case, without psychological complexes or pretension, unwelcoming and hairy; advertising executives and salesmen at fancy stores; enemies of anything that shocks; respectful of authority, they are fans of enlightened capitalism and culture. It's the end of the sordid and grandiose, the comical and the nasty; sadomasochism is now nothing more than a way of dressing for the proper gay man.[27]

As this quote illustrates, a simple reading of *Revue Arcadie* as "clos-eted" and of '80s gay imagery as "out" is misleading. A more accurate understanding of the shift in representations is that *Revue Arcadie*'s images of homosexuals who possessed "dignity" were replaced with images that did nothing to threaten bourgeois norms. While *Arcadie*'s strategy had been transparent, the images of the '80s were not. A veil of '70s autonomy served to mask an underlying message of respect-ability. In *Gai pied hebdo*'s final issue, Joseph-Marie Hulewicz, a former editor, acknowledged the error of the magazine's assimilationist strat-egy, which he described as trying "to adopt a heterosexual, clean and serious, normative and repressive vision of homosexuality. More than anything it was about remaining submissive and resigned and man-aging the space that we had been kindly conceded."[28]

## Apathy and the arrival of AIDS

In the early 1980s, the general consensus among French gay people was that the days of political activism were over. By repealing dis-criminatory laws, the new Socialist government appeared to have met all the demands of gay militants. Consequently, the *raison d'être* for groups like the GLHs and the FHAR had vanished – as had that for Club Arcadie. Not surprisingly, these organizations ceased to exist. When asked the question: "Gay political activism seemed to die out with the legal repeals in the early '80s; were the two events linked?" Jan-Paul Pouliquen, former leader of the CUARH, responded:

Yes of course. As soon as we got the repeal of the laws, well, there was no more discrimination against homosexuality. What could we fight for at the time?…At the time the idea of homosexual marriage or pseudo-marriage didn't interest anyone – it just made people laugh.[29]

In July 1985, *Gai pied* published an article, based upon interviews with men in gay bars in the Marais, that illustrates this point. The article was titled: "Do you get off on politics? Today, militancy is not very 'in'!" Perhaps playing off the potential double meaning of the word "indifference," it began with the observation: "Faced with indifference, gays respond with indifference." It then cited a series of responses that together upheld the widespread notion that the days of militant politics were a thing of the past: "If a guy flirts with me and begins to ask my political opinions, I run." "I come to [gay bars] with friends to talk over drinks in an environment filled with men; we talk about everything except politics." "I come to [gay bars] alone only to pick up guys. What interests me the most are the guy's 'sexual opinions.'" "If you want to pick up a guy, don't talk politics. It's more revolting than a zit on your face!"[30] The expressions of political apathy in these interviews often expressed the notion that political militancy was simply old-fashioned – a particularly damaging criticism in the context of a gay bar in the Marais, where at least the appearance of youth was *de rigueur*. This kind of ridicule against older gay political leaders took various forms, from the subtle to the explicitly *ad hominem*: "We need to put the dinosaurs in the Museum of Prehistory";[31] or "[The CUARH] could use a good face lift!"[32]

Tragically, the apathy in early 1980s coincided with the arrival and spread of AIDS in France, a country where the response to the disease was dreadfully slow. Many have attributed the delay to the weakness of community organization in France; however, the sociologist Frédéric Martel, a strong defender of the French republican model and critic of American-style identity politics, has argued the opposite – that it was precisely because of the existence of a community that French homosexuals were slow to protect themselves from the virus,. Martel's book, *The Pink and the Black*, has been rightly criticized for claiming that blame rests primarily with separatist, ghettoizing leaders in the gay community of the time, who he claims shared a delusional fear of widespread homophobia, which led them to discourage gay men from seeking help from government and medical authorities outside the community: "the spokespersons for militant homosexuality thus refused to see the scope of the pandemic and were unable to respond to the formidable challenge of alerting homosexuals without increasing the stigma. ... They preferred to sacrifice crucial health imperatives in favor of a blind defense of sexual liberation."[33] A critical problem with Martel's analysis is that it ignores the widespread political apathy of the time and misinterprets the politics of the few remaining gay leaders of the time. As David Caron's study of AIDS in France has pointed out,

The few militants still active in the 1980s were, for the most part, former members of the FHAR or the GLHs. They belonged to a tradition that favored the radical subversion of sexual norms rather than the affirmation of a separate identity in what they called a ghetto. The separatist gay community blamed for the spread of AIDS in the early years simply did not exist. If French gays were late in organizing collective responses to the epidemic, it wasn't as Martel claims, because of their misplaced allegiance to a separatist community, which they largely rejected, but precisely because they behaved like good, republican Frenchmen.[34]

Indeed, to the extent that "France could not understand AIDS, an epidemic inseparable from, although not limited to, the existence of marginalized communities," the delayed response in France had less to do with anti-republican, ghettoizing political leaders than with a widespread appreciation for French universalism.[35] In other words, "France applied its own founding narrative of universal equality to HIV itself, as if the virus were able to abide by the 'Declaration of the Rights of Man and the Citizen'."[36] The tragic consequences of an apathy shored up by universalist values serves as a harsh reminder of the ways in which the closet of French republicanism, which in the past had served to protect French homosexuals from more extreme forms of legal censure, can also do harm.

## Pragmatic politics and the 1985 law against discrimination

Despite the prevailing apolitical ethos in the early 80s, the political arena was not entirely empty. One gay political group appears to have survived the 1979–1981 turning point, the CUARH. In addition, several new associations were formed. However, the new organizations, which included *Homosexualité et socialisme*, the *Gais retraités*, and *Gais pour la liberté*, served initially as social spaces rather than as structures for political action. *Homosexualité et socialisme* was a group where left-leaning gays could meet people of the same political tendency, as opposed to some kind of structure for political action. *Gais pour la liberté*, an organization that argued that there is no contradiction between supporting *laissez-faire* economics and being gay, described itself "not as a frustrating militant structure, but rather a place for meeting one another, for imagination, for debates and proposals."[37] Finally, the *Gais retraités* was created primarily in response to the "age-ism" present in other gay meeting spaces, sponsoring social events for its members as well as discussions relevant to the population of older gay men.

In this context, the continued existence of an organization like the CUARH after 1981 was problematic. While it preserved an official legal status, many members withdrew and those who remained lost a sense of purpose. In 1985 the CUARH's leaders, recognizing that the only way to survive was to change, held a membership meeting to discuss the future. The situation was described in an October 1985 issue of *Gai pied hebdo* in an article headlined: *"Le CUARH nouveau est arrivé!"*[38]

> In 1985, what purpose could an "Emergency Committee against the Repression of Homosexuals" possibly serve?...Everyone recognizes that the situation is not the same as before 1981 [when the Socialists arrived in power]. The homophobic laws have disappeared, and the powers of the state appear more understanding toward homosexuals. [But] the CUARH does not want to die.[39]

The author of this article could express with ease the notions that "the situation is not the same as before 1981" and that "the powers of the state appear more understanding." These ideas were floating in the air and given the ease and frequency with which they were used in magazines like *Gai pied hebdo* and in the political discourse of the new associations, were widely understood and accepted as self-evident. While the CUARH stood alone in the early '80s as an advocate for political militancy, after the end of the legal repeals, even its members became unclear about the organization's objectives. Whatever the specific legal and political goals of French gays might be, by 1985 it was clear to at least one patron of a bar in the Marais that the strategies for achieving them would be pragmatic. As he put it, "Gays threw hardcore militancy with its leftist leanings into the dustbin of historical determinism. ... Afterwards, there was something like a big void, and it didn't encourage much of a gay 'community'. ... Now, there's a new militancy, which seems more pragmatic and more open."[40]

In July 1985 the French legislature passed the first of two important pieces of legislation affecting gay people, a law prohibiting discrimination against homosexuals, and in 1999 it passed the second, the *Pacte Civil de Solidarité*, establishing civil unions available to two individuals regardless of their sex. These two laws are fundamentally different from earlier legislation affecting homosexuals in France because they addressed affirmative rights, as opposed to restrictions on gay people's freedom. The 1985 law prohibited discrimination based on an individual's sexual orientation in matters such as housing, employment, and other civil rights.[41] One way of explaining the appearance of this law is stressing that during the 1980s, lawmakers' attitudes had moved toward greater acceptance of homosexuality. While this may be true, it seems that the law's passage was especially due to the success that gay groups had in equating the category of sexual orientation with the more "legitimate" categories of race and gender. As gay political groups appeared more respectable during the '80s, they found themselves in a better position to forge important political alliances with other powerful groups – *SOS Racisme*, feminists, and the Socialist party. Each of these three alliances proved critical to the passage of the 1985 antidiscrimination law.

The alliance with *SOS Racisme* encouraged legislators to think of homosexuality as a category similar to race, that is, an immutable category to which one belongs from birth and a category for which there exists no legitimate reason for discrimination. The importance of this alliance can be seen in discussions of the antidiscrimination law, where the term "anti-homosexual racism" was used instead of the more contemporary term "homophobia."[42] An informal alliance began in late 1984, when leaders of *SOS Racisme* and groups such as *Gais pour la liberté* began meeting to form common strategies. As a result of these meetings, in December 1984 *Gais pour la liberté* published a new charter, which explicitly stated its shared mission: "The work that remains to be done for women, immigrants, *beurs* (i.e., individuals born in France of North African decent), and young people is of equal importance to homosexuals."[43] In June 1985 gay leaders organized a march to support the antidiscrimination law.[44] They chose as the march's slogan "Don't touch my lifestyle," a slight modification of *SOS Racisme*'s slogan, "Don't touch my buddy."[45] Throughout 1985, *Gai pied hebdo* published announcements for *SOS Racisme*, along with invitations to its protests, and *Gai pied hebdo* encouraged its readers to attend so that "homophobia will at last be recognized as a form of racism."[46]

While the antidiscrimination bill was being debated in the national assembly, *SOS Racisme* held a benefit concert to which both its members and members of the gay press and political groups were invited. Malek Boutih, former president of *SOS Racisme*, remembers that "the militants who fought for gay rights were active in our organization. We had, for example, friends at *Gai pied*. Journalists from [the radio station] *Fréquence Gaie* joined us very early. [Their struggle] is thus also part of our history."[47] Soon after the passage of the antidiscrimination law, the new charter of *SOS Racisme* was modified to include the goal of "making public and denouncing every antihomosexual action."[48]

The alliance with feminists was also important, primarily because the law prohibiting discrimination against homosexuals came in the form of an amendment to a law initially aimed at preventing discrimination against women. During the parliamentary debates, supporters of the "anti-sexist" bill, such as the Socialist Deputy Ghislaine Toutain, accepted the additional category of "discrimination based on lifestyle."[49] Finally, the connections with the Socialist party that created the new political group *Homosexualité et Socialisme*, and with Deputy Jean-Pierre Michel, in particular, facilitated the passage of the bill through both the national assembly and the senate.

The bill that was introduced in 1985 was not the first version. In 1981, a bill prohibiting discrimination against "male homosexuals, female homosexuals, or transsexuals" had been introduced.[50] However, when the antidiscrimination bill was re-introduced by Jean-Pierre Michel in 1985, the language was changed to refer to discrimination based on "sexual orientation," leaving out the category of transsexuals. Eventually the reference to "sexual orientation" was also removed and in the final form of the law, the terminology "discrimination based on lifestyle" (in French, *"en raison de moeurs"*) replaced any mention of sexuality. Prior to sponsoring the bill, Jean-Pierre Michel had met with the minister of Justice, Robert Badinter, who suggested that the term "based on lifestyle" would allow the bill to pass more easily.[51] Michel recalls that the strategy of using a broad term like "lifestyle" worked "partly because at the time there had been a trial for someone who was fired because he had long hair ... and [lifestyle] is a term that covers homosexuals among other things."[52] Michel's use of this strategy was clear in his statement to the national assembly, when he said that the amendment "concerns all those who, by their behavior, their lifestyle, their clothing, their haircut, or who knows what, could have a particular service denied to them."[53] By employing the term "based on lifestyle," Michel made an appeal to the legislators' republican notions of universalism, and with the amendment couched in universal terms, rather than in terms referring specifically to sexual orientation, the parliamentary debates were focused less on homosexuality and more on notions of equality.

## The *Pacte civil de solidarité* (PaCS)

The 1990s legislation creating a legally recognized partnership structure available to same-sex couples in the form of the *Pacte Civil de Solidarité* (PaCS) is perhaps the ultimate sign of French gay people's successful assimilation.[54] The idea of some form of legally recognized partnership had come up before, as early as the 1970s, but it was not until the mid-'80s that anyone began to take the idea seriously. The 1970s gay militant Gérard Bach-Ignasse noted the dramatic change in attitudes: "It wasn't until the mid-'80s that the idea of family or of a homosexual partnership became a positive thing. Until then, the gay discourse had always been an anti-family discourse."[55]

The shift in attitudes is linked largely to the spread of AIDS in France in the late '80s and early '90s, when gays were suddenly facing the legal and financial consequences of premature deaths. Jan-Paul Pouliquen, who led the *Collectif pour une union sociale*, the original political movement that fought to establish civil marriage for same-sex couples, remembered the urgency of the situation and explained that his awareness of the consequences of AIDS is what first led him to take an interest in the project of a civil marriage for gay couples. Pouliquen recalls that he read an article in 1991 about "a guy who died of AIDS and his partner was kicked out of the apartment before the cadaver was even cold. I was completely revolted."[56] This revulsion led him to contact Jean-Pierre Michel, the deputy who sponsored the antidiscrimination bill back in 1985 and who remembers that AIDS may have been responsible not only for getting the PaCS bill heard, but also for gaining the sympathies of many lawmakers. He remembers that even those who were most hostile to the bill, "had contacts, sometimes friends, in very difficult situations, and so through some kind of compassion with regard to AIDS, it made things easier."[57]

As soon as Pouliquen, Bach-Ignasse, and Michel began discussions with legislators, they recognized the need for compromise, particularly with regard to the question of adoption. In the first draft of the law, adoption was included among the rights offered; however, this provision was eventually removed and did not appear in the final version of the law. Michel explained its exclusion in terms of political necessity: "There was no point in sinking the boat by overloading it. ... One and half years prior, we tried to reform adoption law in a positive way. ... But [the national assembly] didn't even want to allow heterosexual, non-married couples to adopt, much less lesbian and gay couples."[58] Pouliquen remembers that he conducted surveys and found that only 10 percent of French people had a favorable attitude toward a version that included adoption rights, while 70 percent had a positive attitude that left adoption out: "So, we're not crazy – we're not going to ruin the whole project just for one article."[59]

Recently, with the debates over gay marriage, the issue of adoption has come up again in France. The notion of same-sex families is being discussed with greater frequency and there are signs that attitudes toward gay parents are changing slowly in France. One sign of this change is that a new word, *"homoparentalité"* appeared in the French language in 1997 and in the *Petit Robert* dictionary in 2001.[60] Another is that in 2006, the *Cour de Cassation* held that gay parents may extend parental rights to their partners when it is in the best interest of the child.[61] However, back in the mid-90s, it was clear that despite the desexualized rhetoric surrounding the PaCS, legislators were clearly not willing to allow PaCS couples to adopt. The association of male homosexuality with pederasty and pedophilia that was articulated rather explicitly by some lawmakers had heightened the fears of including adoption in the measure.[62] During the final debates over the PaCS, anti-PaCS protests used slogans such as "One child: one dad and one mom. One child, two dads, that's trouble"; and children carried signs saying "I want a mom and a dad."[63] Gérard Bach-Ignasse remembers the exclusion of adoption as a political necessity: "There wasn't a single deputy who would support adoption for homosexuals. There wasn't even a possibility of discussing it, because of the possible association with pedophilia."[64]

One of the most important characteristics of the final version of the law for the PaCS is that it makes no reference to the sex of the two individuals entering one – the partnership is available to heterosexuals and homosexuals alike; in fact, it is open to any two individuals regardless of their relationship, so long as they are not married or members of the same family. In the early stages of the debate over PaCS, French homosexuals were not in agreement over this issue. There were essentially two camps: the first, led by Jan-Paul Pouliquen, insisted on the universality of a project that could apply equally to same-sex couples, heterosexual couples, but also to two individuals who were not sexually or romantically involved, including "the situation of two old ladies or a priest and his maid"; and the second made up mostly of groups concerned about the effects of AIDS who maintained that the purpose of the project needed to be more than anything the recognition of same-sex couples.[65] In the end, Pouliquen's camp came to dominate the debate. The use of universalist rhetoric in the final draft of the PaCS was particularly important in the context of republican France, where laws must be "indifferent to differences."[66] Pouliquen speaks for many French political activists when he insists that

> Minorities in general cannot resolve their problems as long as they are specifically designated. They killed [sic] Rodney King because he was Black. They deported Jews because they were Jewish…in France, there were 30- 40- 50,000 homosexuals who were deported [sic][67] because of their homosexuality – because the police had kept lists of them…If Jean-Marie Le Pen came to power tomorrow, he would have a list of who is homosexual. That's dangerous. And also, the idea of homosexuals as a different group is not a French way of seeing things.[68]

Phrasing the PaCS in general terms turned out to be a politically effective choice even if some of the rhetoric was disingenuous, given that the main groups pushing for the PaCS were gay and lesbian groups. Yet one of the biggest surprises since the PaCS was enacted in 1999 has been that approximately 60 percent of the couples entering a PaCS have been made up of two people of different sexes.[69]

The universalist, neutral language of the PaCS allowed supporters of the bill to couch the law in terms compatible with the French republican model of assimilation but also to desexualize the debate and to avoid criticisms like those heard in American debates over homosexuality of establishing "special rights" for homosexuals. It is a good example of the elasticity and resiliency of French republican rhetoric and of how in contrast to the relative ineffectiveness of the early '70s calls for radical difference, strategies built on values of universalism and assimilation have proved politically effective for French gay people.

Critics of the PaCS have claimed that it promotes the idea that the heteronormative model of monogamous, two-person, sexual relationships is superior to other forms of human relationships, including friendships, sequential monogamy, and polyamory. The response to this kind of criticism has generally been that those who are not interested in the PaCS, are simply not required to enter one. Jean-Pierre Michel explained:

> I answer that the fact that I propose a law does not force anyone to enter into its framework. The gays and lesbians who want to live in a couple, or who already do, and who want to have a civil partnership, because they expect to share their lives together, they will do it. Those who don't, and who think that it's one of the characteristics of gay life to be able to change partners easily – which by the way would not be impeded by civil partnership – and they don't feel the need to be legally recognized, for their housing for security social, they don't have to. I mean we don't force anyone.[70]

The problem with this kind of response is that it ignores the symbolic power of the PaCS, and focuses instead only on the practical and legal consequences. Symbolically, the availability of a legally recognized partnership structure for homosexual couples grants French homosexuals greater mobility across the social landscape and ultimately increases the speed at which the heterosexual/homosexual binary might fade away. At the same time, the PaCS makes the line between acceptable and unacceptable homosexuality more explicit, and brings issues of sexual-normativity to the foreground. A better response to critics of the PaCS might involve a clearer recognition of their particular concerns, which lie primarily in the realm of the symbolic. Such a response, for example, would provide some assurance for those who are not interested in the PaCS, or more broadly, for those who fall outside of sexual norms, that they will not necessarily be left behind or silenced in the future. Yet at the same time, for many, the creation of the PaCS remains a very subversive act. Socialist deputy, Patrick Bloche explained the PaCS in terms of both normalization and subversion: "The PaCS contests the heterosexual symbolic order...but also reinforces the social archetype of the couple."[71] If nothing else, sexuality is no longer a taboo topic for parliamentary debates, and in the words of the *Garde des Sceaux,* Elisabeth Guigou "No one here in the Parliament will ever openly declare him/herself homophobic again!"[72]

## Since the PaCS

Since the PaCS, gay politics struggles in France have focused on three primary issues: the legal censure of hate speech based on sexual orientation (frequently, referred to as the "anti-homophobia law"), adoption by gay parents, and gay marriage. The questions of adoption and gay marriage have occupied the political scene since the beginning of the 2000s, and though small steps have been made, neither is legally recognized today. The law regarding hate speech against individuals because of their sexual orientation, however, was passed in December 2004.[73] The new measure adds sexual orientation as a category to the text of a law that already punished racist or anti-Semitic hate speech, so that anyone who provokes hatred or violence against someone on the basis sexual orientation can now be punished with up to a year in prison and a fine of 45,000 euros. Defenders of the law have of course insisted on the universalist spirit of the text: "As surprising as it might seem, the notion does not appear in any legal code; our law only speaks of 'sexual orientation.' If someone calls a heterosexual a 'dirty straight', he or she will have the same rights as a gay person who gets called a 'dirty faggot'."[74] Yet, it seems that the strategy of universalist rhetoric in this case was not as successful as it was in the case of the PaCS. In the wake of the law, a strong backlash has developed in recent years, and a new word *"liberticide"* (the death of freedom) has been coined to describe the perceived effect of a law that is "extremely serious for the principle of the equality of all before the Law and dangerously threatens the foundation of our Republic"[75] and establishes a new government agency of "word police."[76] In the end the backlash against the anti-homophobia law demonstrates the continued importance of the universalist rhetoric of French republicanism in political debates. Even supporters of the law recognize that the drafters of the law may not have paid enough attention to the need to couch their demands in universalist terms and fear that the law may actually set back the cause of protecting gays and lesbians:

> It has cost gay people dearly and continues to cost them dearly. From now on, most people will believe that lesbians and gays have at their disposal some kind of privilege when they are victims of defamation or hate speech: many imagine that someone who attacks a gay person will be punished more harshly than someone who attacks a straight person. And some of them add things like, it's better to be gay than straight, Jewish than Catholic, black than white, foreign than French.... [In their minds] the only person who is not protected is the average French guy: straight, white, Catholic.[77]

This chapter began with the period of the repeals of the discriminatory laws in the early 80s and the ways in which French homosexuals began to create a new space for themselves, a space that in many ways was better than the one they had just come out of. Then with the discussions of the antidiscrimination law and the PaCS, the focus shifted to the political effectiveness of assimilationist politics and to the impressive legal changes that resulted. From these discussions, it is possible to see the ways in which the new strategies proved politically effective for French lesbians and gays, especially in contrast to the political ineffectiveness of 70s radicalism. The history of recent legal changes, including the antidiscrimination law in 1985 and the PaCS in 1999, demonstrate that it was not until compromise and assimilationist representations of homosexuality became acceptable as political strategies that positive, legal change occurred.

However, this chapter has also focused on the ways in which the more respectable face of homosexuality created new limitations and reproduced some form of "closet." This change in self-representations by French gays and lesbians raises the question of whether it was public opinion of homosexuality or the meaning of what it is to be homosexual that underwent greater change in those years. Despite the impressive legal changes since the early 1980s, there is some reason to doubt that widespread social attitudes toward subversive sexual and gender roles and toward difference in general changed radically in France during this time, to the extent that gays' self-representations merely came more into alignment with the republic's longstanding requirements for assimilation and acceptance.

# 4
## "Outing" the French Gay Media (The 1990s and 2000s)[1]

Since the 1980s, strategies of assimilation stemming from the universalist discourse of French republicanism have shaped the character of political demands as well as the nature of the resulting legal reforms. In this final chapter, the focus is on the influence of republican universalist rhetoric on gay media from the 1990s through the 2000s, a period that has been marked more by media messages than any other since the Second World War. More specifically, this final chapter turns to three contemporary media sources, the magazine *Têtu*, the magazine *Préférences*, and the French television station PinkTV, for its analysis of the ways in which interiorized forms of self-control continue to influence contemporary French gays' self-representations and prevent them from asserting difference even in their own media.

In this first decade of the twenty-first century, the influence of French universalism remains alive and well – evidenced perhaps not so much by individuals' practices and choices, as by their rhetoric. The analysis that follows demonstrates how republican values, which in earlier decades had protected French homosexuals from more extreme forms of legal censure, can also restrain by compelling French gay media to embrace French universalism – in the specific cases of these three media sources, this means that though their target audiences have been gay men, they all have felt the need to claim that they are serving other, broader audiences:

> The ideal is to have one-third gay boys, one-third gay girls and one-third straight viewership.[2] (Pierre Garnier, PinkTV's Director of Marketing)

> It is a mistake to make homosexuality into a mission; each of us is too complicated to define ourselves only by a sexual practice.[3] (Editorial, *Préférences*, Issue 1)

> Until now there were lesbian magazines and there were magazines for gay men ... As of now, there is *Têtu*.[4] (Editorial, *Têtu* magazine, Issue 1)

The goal here is to expose the true identities of these media sources. Since its inception in 1995, *Têtu* has claimed to serve both lesbians and gay men. The first few issues of the magazine aimed for a balance between articles for men and articles for women and were moderately successful in achieving this goal. However, this strategy ended abruptly after the third issue, and though the magazine continues to call itself "the magazine of gay men and lesbians," only 3 percent of its readers today are lesbians and virtually none of the content is intended for them.[5] A similar story can be told about *Préférences*, a magazine for "metrosexuals," that claims to be for men regardless of their sexuality, though it is clear from its content that the editors are working on the assumption that there are no heterosexual readers. Finally, there is PinkTV. Since its creation in 2004, PinkTV has gone the furthest in aligning its description of itself with the ideals of French universalism, asserting that it is a serious cultural channel for everyone, gay or straight, male or female. The channel has striven to provide programming for a wide demographic range with a good dose of high culture, even though it seems to have been clear to everyone appearing on the station that its primary audience was composed of gay men looking to have fun. For each of these media sources, the distance between its content and the description it made of itself began small and then grew over time as the content was increasingly shaped by the need to satisfy its core audience of gay men looking for lighthearted entertainment.

An obvious question is why these media sources have bothered trying to present themselves as something other than what their content would indicate. Media scholars have a term for the distance between the desirable (that which a person should want, as defined by a particular culture's norms) and the desired (that which a person actually wants): they call it the "value paradox."[6] The desirable and the desired can coincide, but when they do not, marketers face the difficult task of communicating to potential consumers that they will get what they want (the desired) without being too incongruent with predominant social values (the desirable). In these cases, the ideal marketing strategy will mask the desired quality with a representation of the desirable. An example is a car that happens to be luxurious (the desired), but whose advertising focuses on its safety features (the desirable), allowing a person who wants to be perceived as practical and prudent to be a bit frivolous and purchase a fancy car with less fear of social disapproval.

The existence of value paradoxes means that an individual's behavior does not always reflect what is desirable in a particular culture, and an awareness of value paradoxes in a particular society can be a useful tool in examining cultural difference. In some places – marketers tend to cite Asian countries as examples – respect for tradition is valued (the desirable), even though individuals might seek innovation (the desired). In the United States, the values of freedom and independence correspond to the desirable, though there is evidence that a sense of belonging represents the desired. In France, an appreciation of high culture and serious thinking along with the ideals of universalism embodied in the French republican model are all components of the *desirable*, though being entertained and belonging to a community of people who resemble you may be what is often actually *desired*.

The cases of *Têtu, Préférences,* and PinkTV all illustrate the distance between the desirable and desired for French gays. These various media sources have worked hard to portray themselves in a way that conveys an air of seriousness and conforms to the *desirable* French republican model of universalism and assimilation, while at the same time delivering the content *desired* by a core audience of gay men looking to be entertained. In the end, the cases of *Têtu, Préférences,* and PinkTV show that though French gay people might opt for the sectarian in their media choices, the republican discourse of universalism remains nevertheless seductive.

## *Têtu* magazine pretends it is for lesbians

The early 1990s saw the end of the mythical *Gai pied hebdo*, which printed its last issue in 1992. Despite the distance between *Gai pied hebdo*'s description of itself as a serious, politically engaged magazine and the reality of its content, there was one aspect of the magazine about which the editors were totally up front. Unlike *Têtu*, the magazine that would come to dominate the gay media landscape of the 1990s, *Gai pied hebdo* was open about its decision to be a magazine only for men. In a letter to the editor from the magazine's early days, "Laurent" was angry, not only because none of the magazine's editors were women, but also because lesbian issues were not represented in the magazine at all. *Gai pied* responded to his letter this way: "Putting together a magazine project like these first three issues does not seem to interest lesbians right now. Instead, they seem to be creating their own press and that seems very positive. Of course, we could have asked some of our lesbian friends to write something for us, but that would have been a false inclusiveness, a shameless use of tokens."[7] The use of tokens in more recent media forms, including the magazine *Têtu,* but also more recently with PinkTV, has not been subject to such scrutiny.

The void left by the disappearance of *Gai pied hebdo* was eventually filled in 1995 by the new monthly magazine, *Têtu,* which aimed to be the new magazine for both gay men and lesbians. The first issues of the magazine did try to represent both men and women and made an effort to give considerable space to political issues. However, a glance at the covers of the magazine over the last ten years reveals that a lot has changed. A woman has not graced the cover of *Têtu* since 2001 and the faces of political figures and celebrities have been replaced with naked torsos of young, good-looking men.

*Têtu,* which sold a mere 10,000 copies in 1997, eventually attained financial stability with 50,000 copies sold per month in 2004.[8] For the first time, a gay magazine was able to procure mainstream advertisers, including ads for bottled waters, internet service providers, French perfume companies, and fashion designers (the magazine was originally financed by the group Yves Saint Laurent). Reactions to the first issue were mixed. Some were happy to find a decent, respectable magazine: "At last a gay magazine that you can read in the metro...."[9] But the main issue on readers' minds was the decision to make a magazine for both gay men and lesbians:

> "I have found what I was missing so much: a magazine made as much for girls as for boys." (Valérie )[10]

> "Your magazine has promised a lot: finally a magazine for homosexuals, men and women." (Nicole R.)[11]

> "I don't like the idea of including gays and lesbians (I don't read the articles for lesbians – a part of the magazine for them just means fewer pages for gay men)." (Jean-Claude )[12]

*Têtu* responded to these readers:

> Not easy to satisfy everyone... Yes, the first issue of *Têtu* was not perfect. No, we could not treat all the subjects that you want from us. Have patience... lesbian readers will see that this month they are not forgotten.[13]

The content of *Têtu*'s first issues resembled its description and hopes for itself more closely than it did in its later issues. The second issue was particularly balanced, with the main story titled, "Everything boys who love boys think they know about girls who love girls and vice versa," announced on the cover along with the image of a half-male, half-female head. By the third issue, however, the editorial staff seems to have lost patience with the mounting criticism from lesbian readers and published this rather patronizing statement scolding them for their lack of understanding:

> Girls, stop counting the number of pages that we publish about you and consider the number of topics that are for both gay men and lesbians. And then, be patient: we are preparing articles that you've never read anywhere else.[14]

It turned out that readers, both male and female, had to be extraordinarily patient. *Têtu* temporarily and unexpectedly ceased publication for seven months between the third and fourth issues. When the fourth issue finally came out, the magazine had chosen to abandon its mission of being a magazine for lesbians and gay men, a choice that pleased some readers:

> After rediscovering *Têtu*, I noticed that improvements have been made and that it's going in the direction I had wished for (and apparently I wasn't the only one): abandoning ambiguity, giving up on the idea of including lesbians. (Jean-Claude)[15]

And disappointed others:

> When I first learned that your magazine had come out, I ran to get it! But now, I'm a disappointed reader. Where are the women? You were the only ones to aim for inclusiveness: now who will do it? -(Ségolène[16])

In addition to the controversy over the question of lesbians, the magazine has faced a second tension between providing serious information versus entertainment.[17] Didier Lestrade, who cofounded the magazine with Pascal Loubet, explained the magazine's double mission by stating that "*Têtu* is the descendant of *Gai pied*, while at the same time being its opposite. It has pursed its mission of information and political engagement, while at the same time being, and why not, a futile magazine."[18] Thus, the magazine opted for something in-between.

Over the years, *Têtu*, has moved further from its idealized description of itself. Since 1995, the magazine has continued to allow the space devoted to serious information to cede the way to more frivolous entertainment. More significantly perhaps, it has virtually abandoned its mission of being a magazine for both gay men and lesbians. With regard to the balance of serious information and frivolous entertainment, the chart (Figure 4.1) shows the extent to which the amount of space devoted to "hard news" (information on politics, legal issues, history, science, literature, and other forms of high culture) has been replaced with "soft news" (information that is more entertainment-oriented, including topics such as shopping, cooking, travel, exercise, beauty, erotica, places to go out, humor, love advice, horoscopes, celebrities). The percentages

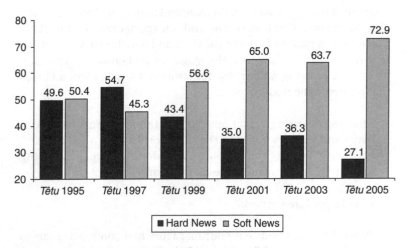

*Figure 4.1*   Relative seriousness of *Têtu* over time (%)

*Note*: Information on the methodology for Figure 4.1 is in endnote 19, p. 143.

listed in Figure 4.1 represent the percentage of the entire magazine's space devoted to each type of news overtime.[19]

Another indication of this shift (Figure 4.2) is the substantial increase in the percentage of the magazine's space devoted to selling products, either in the form of advertising or in the form of products exhibited in noncritical "reviews."

*Têtu* knows what it is doing. Perhaps it started out trying to be serious, because that is what its editors and writers had hoped for in a magazine, but since then *Têtu* has been getting less serious, because this is what its readers want. A survey conducted in 2005 confirms this, stating that "readers especially appreciate the esthetic quality of the magazine, more than the style and the originality of the articles. Advertising is also well received: 87% of the readers judge that it suits the magazine well."[20] In the same poll, 77 percent of readers said that *Têtu* dedicates either the right amount or not enough of its space to sex and erotica.[21]

With respect to the issue of being a magazine for both gay men and lesbians, the editors continue to maintain a gender-neutral discourse,

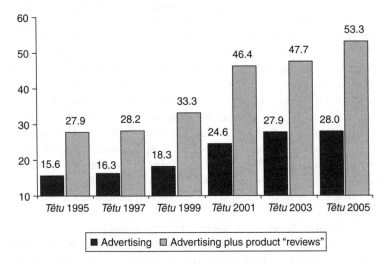

*Figure 4.2* Percentage of space devoted to advertising in *Têtu*[a]

*Note:* [a] The data for this chart come from a sampling of 6 issues of *Têtu* magazine made up of the September issues for 1995, 1997, 1999, 2001, 2003, and 2005. For each issue, I determined the number of 1/12ths of a page devoted to articles, explicit advertising, and less explicit kinds of advertising in the form of noncritical product "reviews."

though the magazine has clearly become a magazine almost entirely for gay men. In April 2005, Thomas Doustaly, the editor of *Têtu*, participated in an online chat. When someone asked him why the magazine is more dedicated to gay men than to lesbians, he responded by saying that this simply is not the case:

> You cannot say that *Têtu* is more dedicated to gay men. On the contrary, when I arrived [as editor] in October 1997, I chose to add "the gay and lesbian magazine" to *Têtu's* title, even though for more than a year before, the preceding team had thought it needed to be a strictly gay male magazine in order to succeed. Since then, the editorial policy has not varied.[22]

The amount of space devoted to lesbian readers (both advertising space and space for articles) has varied over time, with four distinct periods: the first period (issues one through three) when the editors hoped to produce a magazine that would attract both gay male and lesbian readers; the second period, in 1996 and 1997 when the strategy of including lesbians was completely abandoned; the third period in 1998 and 1999, when the amount of space devoted to lesbians increased; and the fourth period from 2000 to the present when the number of articles for lesbians dropped sharply, to levels even lower than the second period when the magazine did not even claim to serve lesbians. The temporary increase in articles for lesbians in 1998 and 1999 can be largely attributed to the sharp increase in the number of articles discussing the proposed law for civil unions for same-sex couples (the PaCS) that passed in 1999. During the two years preceding its passage, articles covered the legal and political battles in detail, but there was also a surge in the number of articles concerned with couples in general (Table 4.1). These kinds of articles account for most of the increase in lesbian representation during those years.[23]

Since 2000, however, it seems that the magazine has resigned itself to being a magazine almost exclusively for gay men.[24] Though the cover still states that *Têtu* is the "magazine of gay men and lesbians," the last time that a woman appeared on the cover was with issue number 53 in February 2001, and since then, the cover has always had a man on it – and for only four issues was he wearing a shirt.

*Table 4.1* Proportion of *Têtu* devoted to lesbians (1995–2006)

|  | % of articles for lesbians[a] | % of advertising for lesbians[b] | Ratio of articles for gay men to articles for lesbians | Ratio of ads for gay men to ads for lesbians |
|---|---|---|---|---|
| **Strategy of balance** 1995 (issues 1–3) | 19.2 | 7.6 | 2.2 to 1 | 7.7 to 1 |
| **Strategy of no lesbians** 1996–1997 | 7.0 | 0.8 | 6.3 to 1 | 70.6 to 1 |
| **Pre-PaCS** 1998–1999 | 19.6 | 6.5 | 1.8 to 1 | 6.7 to 1 |
| **Post-PaCS** 2000–2006 | 4.7 | 2.3 | 8.4 to 1 | 19.0 to 1 |
| **Overall** 1995–2006 | **9.8** | **4.2** | **4.0 to 1** | **11.5 to 1** |

*Notes*:

[a] These figures represent the amount of space devoted to articles written specifically for lesbians plus one half of the space devoted to articles written deliberately for both gay men and lesbians, expressed as a percentage of the total space devoted to articles. The remaining space includes articles for gay men as well as articles whose readers' gender and sexual identities are undeterminable or irrelevant.

[b] These figures represent the amount of space devoted to advertising made specifically for lesbians plus one half of the space devoted to advertising made deliberately for both gay men and lesbians, expressed as a percentage of the total space devoted to advertising. The remaining space includes advertising for gay men as well as advertising whose targets' gender and sexual identities are undeterminable or irrelevant.

Information on the methodology for Tables 4.1, 4.2, and 4.3 is in endnote 23, p. 143.

The strategy of abandoning lesbian readers makes some sense when one considers the number of lesbians who read the magazine (Table 4.2). There are various ways of estimating the number of lesbian readers: one of which is to look at the results of surveys published in *Têtu*. Others include calculating the relative amount of space devoted to advertisements and articles of interest to each population, or comparing the number of personals written by gay men to the number written by lesbians.

It is hard to make the argument that *Têtu* has not tried to appeal to lesbian readers, since according to Table 4.2, the percentage of space

*Table 4.2*   Estimated percentage of male and female readers of *Têtu*

|  | Articles[a] | Ads[b] | Survey[c] | Personals[d] |
|---|---|---|---|---|
| % gay male | 39.1 | 48.7 | 88 | 90 |
| % lesbian | 9.8 | 4.2 | 3 | 10 |
| Ratio (gay male to lesbian) | 4 to 1 | 11.5 to 1 | 29.3 to 1 | 9 to 1 |

*Notes:*
[a]The remaining 51 percent of space devoted to articles could not be identified as specifically intended for heterosexuals or homosexuals.
[b]The advertising figure listed here for gay men includes advertisements specifically targeting gay male readers plus one half of the advertisements deliberately targeting both gay male and lesbian readers. Likewise, the figure for lesbians includes advertisements specifically targeting lesbian readers plus one half of the advertisements deliberately targeting both gay male and lesbian readers. The remaining 47.1 percent of space devoted to advertising could not be identified as specifically targeting heterosexuals or homosexuals.
[c]The study, which was based on 1000 questionnaires received in the spring of 2005, indicated that 88 percent of *Têtu*'s readers identify themselves as gay male, 3 percent as lesbian, 6 percent as bisexual, 2 percent as heterosexual, and 1 percent did not respond to the question. 96 percent of the respondents were male and 4 percent were female ("Etude TNS Sofrès-*Têtu*," 79).
[d]This figure comes from the September 2000 issue of *Têtu* (no. 48, pages 100–5), which had 25 personals from women looking for women, 208 from men looking for men, and 5 other types of personals; and the September 1999 issue (no. 37, pages 87–91), which had 12 personals from women looking for women, 125 from men looking for men, and 3 other types of personals.

devoted to articles for lesbian readers far exceeds estimates of the percentage of readers who are lesbian. For example, while the ratio of gay male to lesbian articles is 4 to 1, the ratio of gay men to lesbians who responded to a 2005 survey was 29.3 to 1, which would indicate that the magazine has potentially amplified the importance of its lesbian readers by 633 percent (Table 4.3).

The importance of achieving a fair balance between articles for gay men and for lesbians occupies an important place in statements from the magazine's editors. Critics are simply dismissed for making unreasonable demands, as illustrated in this defense from Didier Lestrade, a cofounder of the magazine: "We want more lesbians, but until they get exactly half, certain lesbians will be angry."[25] In the summer of 2000, *Têtu* launched a new magazine for its lesbian readers, *Têtu Madame*. The first issue of *Têtu Madame* turned out to be

Table 4.3 Amplification of the importance of *Têtu's* lesbian readers

|  | Ads | Survey | Personals |
|---|---|---|---|
| **Ratio of gay men to lesbians in ads, survey, and personals** | 11.5 to 1 | 29.3 to 1 | 9 to 1 |
| **Ratio of gay male to lesbian articles** | 4 to 1 | 4 to 1 | 4 to 1 |
| *Amplification of the importance of lesbians in allocating article space* | +188% | +633% | +125% |

also its last, and judging from readers' letters to the editor, the tone of the magazine had been simply too frivolous:

> The two of us read issue one. ... Perhaps we are too old (30 and 38 years old), too poor, too stupid or too out of style, but we really found this magazine too urban (even Parisian) too hip and too rich (a just a bit contemptuous). (Marlène and Karine)[26]

Four years later, the editors made a second attempt to attract lesbian readers. *Têtue*, a special six-page section dedicated to lesbians, began appearing in May 2004. Its presence has, however, not fundamentally changed the magazine's character. In 2005, a reader wrote, "*Têtu* the 'magazine for gays and lesbians'? ... Please excuse me for a second, but the articles [for lesbians] in the *Têtue* section start on page 117 ... with 116 pages before that dedicated to gay men."[27] The editors of *Têtu* responded with: "116 pages dedicated to gay men, oh really? Most of the subjects treated in *Têtu* are for everyone. For example, the film from André Téchiné, *Les temps qui changent, Alexander* from Oliver Stone, Irshad Manji, the Sistine Chapel, k.d. lang ... but also culture pages, news, recipes, a report on relations between gay men and lesbians, the pastor who became a porn star. ... The only pages dedicated uniquely to gay men were the porn page and the beauty section."[28]

An important sign of *Têtu's* failure to attract lesbian readers was the creation of a separate magazine for lesbians in 2003, called *La 10ème Muse*. In an obvious reference to *Têtu's* overwhelming gay male aesthetic and hypocritical label of itself as the "magazine of gay men and lesbians," the editor of *La Dixième Muse*, Peggy Deweppe, explained the reason for creating the magazine, "*La Dixième Muse* came about because we are sick of looking at guys' asses on glossy paper!"[29]

The question remains then of why *Têtu*'s editors feel the need to continue to claim that the magazine is for lesbians. Strangely enough, it seems to have less to do with satisfying lesbian readers than with satisfying its gay male readers who are attracted to the description of a magazine for both men and women. It is quite telling for example that in a recent poll, despite the fact that only 3 percent of the survey's respondents identified themselves as lesbian, 51 percent were critical of the magazine for "not dedicating enough space to lesbians."[30] Indeed, it seems that everyone would prefer a magazine that avoids catering to a particular community, including a lesbian reader who was interviewed for the 100th anniversary of the magazine: "I am happy that there is the '*Têtue*' section [for lesbians], even though I would never buy an exclusively lesbian magazine. I read the news. The regular columns, the reviews and the articles about famous people provide an interesting point of view without confining themselves to homosexuality."[31]

## *Préférences* magazine pretends that sexual orientation is irrelevant

> Claiming a sexual identity, if such an act is legitimate at all, should never be done just because you have been rejected by society. There is a risk of falling into an absurd system that will reproduce itself forever: social exclusion leads to communitarianism and communitarianism leads to exclusion.[32]

*Préférences Mag*, the "magazine of new genders," avoids saying explicitly who its readers are. The magazine's title implies an editorial affinity for the term "sexual *preference*" as opposed to "sexual *orientation*," suggesting the possibility for less rigidly constructed sexual identities. Indeed, the original idea for the magazine was based on the notion that "to be homosexual or heterosexual is not an attribute of one's life but merely a practice and a sexual preference. What matters is to be in harmony with one's life choices and interests."[33] This is quite different from the description that its American equivalent, *Genre Magazine*, makes of itself: "*Genre* is the complete lifestyle sourcebook for gay men."[34]

The editorial of *Préférences Mag*'s first issue distanced itself from the category of homosexuality, and attempted to depict itself as potentially queer:

Today more than ever, it is necessary to transcend categories and to refuse simplistic clichés. ... We aim to mix up ideological discourses, to instate romantic disorder, to play passionately with our sexuality in a process of constant mixing, to undermine the power relations that limit choices to those of the minority or of the majority, and to refuse uniform ways of thinking.[35]

It claimed to be for readers, both heterosexual and homosexual, who were looking for an alternative to hyper-masculinity, to machismo: "The return of a visible and violent machismo is making it more necessary than ever to expose the situation where all [gender and sexual] roles gravitate around the macho model and enslave all of us, whether we are heterosexual or homosexual, to their hegemony."[36] But was the magazine in any way queer? After reading the first issue's editorial on page 3, one needed merely look at the next few pages to realize that there was nothing queer about *Préférences Mag*. The magazine's imagery is classic, gay, white, male. Any doubt about the intended readership would be eliminated by page 20, which begins a six-page photo spread of half-dressed male models, followed by 14 more pages of nearly naked soccer players. The magazine would have certainly disappointed any readers anticipating "constant mixing," "romantic disorder," and a refusal of "simplistic clichés."

In fact, *Préférences Mag* lacks any glimmer of queer political radicalism, particularly through its frank endorsement of blatant consumerism. An article that talks about creams for making skin look younger, for example, relieves readers of the guilt they might experience from self-indulgent shopping: "To seduce means to offer yourself as a visual object and to get pleasure from it. After decades of dry political militancy when people were always talking about alienation, about refusing to objectify bodies, we have been terrorized by the extreme feminism of the temple's guardians who launched their anathemas from fancy cafés or from television talk shows. We have finally reached a time where we can get rid of our guilt and claim our right to seduce."[37]

Indeed, the magazine endorses some unexpectedly traditional values. In an odd article, entitled "We have so much to be happy for," readers learn about a survey of French people's values at the beginning of the twenty-first century. The article's tone is surprisingly upbeat as it announces the return of family values in what appears to be an unsarcastic tone:

> 21st century, here we are! Long live the family! It's time for the grand return of traditions!... Farewell multicolored scarves, Indian jewelry that we liked so much in the 1970s, running naked in fields of flowers, making love by the sea.... The 60s generation had its time. Today, the defense of traditional values is back in force.[38]

In the end, it seems that the magazine's references to blurred identities, new genders, or sexual experimentation have less to do with radical sexual politics than with a respect for French universalism – to talk in terms of blurred identities has helped the magazine avoid criticism for being a communitarian publication serving gay men specifically. The magazine's reverence for republican values is apparent, for example, in an article from the third issue titled "Let's Create a New Norm," which proclaims that "identity politics are incompatible with equality. Our society is moving toward a legal universal, that is, toward equal rights, and not toward a system based on identity politics that would actually serve to deny the diversity of individuals."[39]

In 2005, the magazine took an important step toward outing itself when it changed its name from *Préférences Mag: The magazine of new genders* to *Préf: The magazine of our preferences* beginning with issue number eight. With this change in its title came a shift toward more explicitly gay male content, which was noticeable immediately in the imagery of the magazine's covers. The covers of the first eight issues showed either a man's face or fully clothed male bodies. As of issue nine, *Préf* adopted the *Têtu*-style imagery of bare-chested men who now appear on every issue's cover. Similarly, while the headlines on the covers of the first seven issues demonstrated a desire to be a magazine not only for metrosexuals regardless of sexuality but also a forum for serious debate of social issues, beginning with issue nine, the covers are all about sex, and explicitly gay sex at that. In the months following the title change, cover titles included "The saga of gay serial killers – a descent into the sexual underworld;"[40] "Special report: male prostitutes, pleasure boys: 'I am not an object, I am a full person',"" (accompanied by a photograph of a bare-chested, sexy man sucking on a popsicle);[41] "An X-rated summer: sex, sex and more sex!"[42]

The question of why the editors of *Préf* bother hiding the fact that the magazine is for gay men has a simple answer – like in the case of *Têtu*, a magazine that refuses to come out as gay seems to be precisely what *Préf*'s readers want:

> I was pleasantly surprised to discover in your pages, a magazine that is less communitarian, less sectarian and especially more ironic about the Scene than I expected.[43] (Anthony)

> Finally an intelligent magazine that is not exclusively for gay men and avoids all the clichés that would come with that (saunas, hundreds of bare chests and articles without interest), but instead, is open to the world.[44] (Jean)

## PinkTV pretends it is for everyone

> Our channel is not just for gays. ... It's a lifestyle channel, so we can be interesting for straight people, too.[45]
> 
> Pascal Houzelot, President of PinkTV

In November 2004, a new station, PinkTV, appeared on French cable television, describing itself as "a channel with a broad scope that blends culture with glamour. It is for gay girls and boys and for all those who feel like watching a different kind of TV built around freedom, tolerance, humor and seduction."[46] The creation of PinkTV and other television stations built around group identities in recent years (including Berbère TV, KTO for Catholics, TFJ for the Jewish community, BeurTV, CorsicaTV, and TVBreizh for Bretons) is particularly surprising in the context of France, a place where political actors and theorists have not embraced identity politics with the same enthusiasm as their American counterparts. The approval of these stations by the *Conseil supérieur de l'audiovisuel* has sparked controversy, in particular from groups like the *Observatoire du communautarisme*, though none of these new stations has provoked more debate than PinkTV. Unlike criticism of the gay station Logo in the United States, the fiercest condemnation of PinkTV has not come "from religious groups but from people outraged...at the efforts of a group to set itself apart."[47]

In descriptions of itself, PinkTV has faced the difficult task of explaining that its content is for gays, lesbians, and people who are "gay-friendly," while at the same time avoiding any association with multiculturalism or American-style identity politics.[48] As a number of recent works have pointed out, the use of "America" in France has generally been more of a rhetorical device than a reflection of reality, since "America" is a word that can be filled with many different meanings, or to borrow the terminology of Levi-Strauss: "America" is a floating signifier. In discussing the use of "America" in France, Eric Fassin has referred to the rhetorical strategy of the American "scarecrow," which involves associating one side of a debate with the "American position," thereby making it impossible to accept without being suspected of betraying France.[49] Or as Denis Provencher explains, "French citizenship is tied to republican universalism, and the French homosexual citizen will often request recognition in the eyes of the family and the state through notions of 'Frenchness' and sameness (ordinariness) instead of difference."[50]

In this context, some sense might be made of PinkTV's enigmatic descriptions of itself. According to the channel's president, Pascal Houzelot, PinkTV is not "a *'communautaire'* station, but an *'identitaire'* station."[51] Given that these two French words are both commonly used interchangeably to refer to political strategies that emphasize the need for political mobilization around distinct identities, it is not clear what he means by this distinction. One possible interpretation is that *"communautaire"* would imply some effort to build a sense of community, while *"identitaire"* merely encourages individual viewers to see something of themselves in the programming, without any calls for group action. It is telling for example to consider PinkTV's slogan of *"liberté, égalité, télé,"* where the missing word is *"fraternité."*

According to an article in *L'Humanité*, the channel "has as its main target gays and lesbians, but it refuses to accept the label of *'communautaire'.'"* The article adds, "Pascal Houzelot prefers to use the term *'identitaire.'* The difference? [Houzelot explains:] 'Our programming is broad. But what brings us together is our tastes.' To preempt any criticism, he adds: 'we will engage ourselves without being militant. The channel will avoid a uniform discourse, which would be contrary to the idea of a space for discussion. This channel appears at the right moment, because society is ready to understand a new reality'."[52]

One reason that PinkTV has been able to use these terms in confusing ways is that the difference in the terms' meanings has not been firmly established by French lexicographers. The word *"communautaire"* is defined in various dictionaries as describing "someone who by principle or by idealism displays him/herself as a part of a community;"[53] "related to living with others; a person who practices or recommends living with others;"[54] or simply "related to a community."[55] In addition to these official sources, native French participants in online forums have offered the following explanations:

- *"Communautarisme* deals with communities, racial or sexual for instance. It is the attitude that some of them have, to 'ghetto' themselves instead of trying to get integrated and mingled with the rest of society."[56]
- "Anglo-Saxon *'communautarisme'* is something we don't want and something we see often in Great Britain and which shows itself externally when a police officer wears a turban or a school teacher wears an [Islamic] veil."[57]
- "For instance, I can say that the appearance of PinkTV, the new gay TV channel is something I don't like because it only accentuates gay *'communautarisme.'* I'd prefer that straight TV stations make less of a big deal out of it and include gays in their programs like normal people."[58]
- "[*Communautarisme*] does not really exist in France. We don't use it to classify people according to their religions, sexuality or tastes (although this trend is slowly appearing), which we think must remain in the private circle."[59]

Determining the meaning of *identitaire*, however, is much more challenging, particularly since the word cannot be found in virtually any dictionary.[60] In fact, only one, the 6-volume *Grand Robert*, includes the word, which it defines as "that which is related to the identity (of a person, of a group)," where identity can mean one of three things; first, as a general term meaning "belonging to a group and feeling it;" second, as a psychological term meaning "the character of that which remains identical to itself"; or third, as a term of formal logic that refers to "the relation in the logical sense between two identical terms."[61] Clearly with regard to PinkTV's use of the term, only the first definition is pertinent. In which case, *"identitaire"* would mean "that which is related to belonging to a group and feeling it." In other words, it would be defined in much the same way as *"communautaire."*

Given the absence of the word *identitaire* in virtually all dictionaries, other less official sources of information might be used to provide some insight into the word's meaning, including the French *Wikipedia*, which combines the two terms, providing a single entry for both. It defines *"communautarisme identitaire"* as "an *identitaire/ communautaire* reaction that considers the community to be more important than the individual.... *Communautarisme identitaire* is a way of thinking that developed in the 1970s and 80s in Anglo-Saxon countries. It turns the value of one's (ethnic, religious, cultural, social, political, mystical, athletic...) community into a value as important, if not more important, than the 'universal' values of freedom and equality."[62]

The confusion over these two words' meanings has allowed PinkTV to fill them with any meanings it wants. Consequently, rather than relying on dictionaries to make sense of PinkTV's descriptions of itself, it is perhaps most constructive to look at the language the station's representatives have used to describe the channel in order to understand the distinction they hope to make between *communautaire* and *identitaire*.

- "Without forgetting to be proud of who we are, we must offer programs larger than that which brings us together."[63]
- "PinkTV is an eclectic channel 'made for a broader public than the gay community, a place for people who love opera or certain cult TV series. ... It will be a station that is involved in the world, without being militant."[64]
- "PinkTV's programming is for all audiences who link unity with diversity, community with plurality, identity with difference."[65]
- PinkTV is the meeting place for gays and gay friendly people who want a new way of looking at the world. Debates, series, interviews...PinkTV will offer its subscribers the opportunity to

reconcile humor with seriousness, involvement with lightness, the classical with the avant-garde... a mix of genres that could serve as the new example of cultural diversity *à la française*."[66]

From statements like these it seems that PinkTV would like its viewers to understand the two terms in the following ways (Table 4.4).

"*Le Set*," the centerpiece of PinkTV programming, which has aired every evening during the channel's first two seasons, is presented in the form of a news magazine. The initial hope was that it would be in the spirit of respected cultural and political programs such as "*Nulle part ailleurs*" and "*Rive droite/Rive gauche*."[67] The show's description explains that "[t]he goal is not to make news by gays, on gays and for gays. Instead, the show will deal with topics that interest us and involve us," according to its head editor Jean-François Lacoux.[68] One of the show's two anchors, Christophe Beaugrand explains that "[t]he show will have a gay identity, without necessarily making any demands."[69] The other co-host, Marie Labory, adds that, "[c]ultural topics will dominate, but we also want to have fun."[70] When asked if the show was exclusively for a gay audience, Labory answered, "[n]o, not at all. That would not be very interesting."[71] As these quotes illustrate, *Le Set's* descriptions of itself exemplify the channel's tension between the desire to exploit a new market niche and the need to avoid being perceived as either "ghettoizing" or stemming from American-style multiculturalism.

Houzelot has talked about developing joint projects with the American gay channel Logo. However, a spokesperson for Logo explained that his channel does not share PinkTV's programming

*Table 4.4*  *Communautaire* versus *identitaire*

| Communautaire | Identitaire |
| --- | --- |
| A single, comprehensive identity | Identity constructed *à la carte* |
| More "American" | Less "American" |
| Ghettoizing, clannish, separatist | French first, discreet about difference |
| Ideological | Individual |
| Identity as a political, public matter | Identity as a private matter |
| Based on sexuality | Based on shared cultural tastes |
| Old-fashioned | New and trendy |

tastes, since "Logo is for self-identified gay or lesbian viewers who are out in their community."[72] Indeed, it is revealing to compare PinkTV's description with Logo's, which has no difficulty stating that it is specifically for a lesbian and gay audience: "For the first time ever, Gay America has a home on television where we can go to see ourselves.... Logo is the channel for Gay America."[73] Yet despite the difference in the two channels' descriptions of themselves, PinkTV's programming is beginning to resemble Logo's more and more, as PinkTV continues to increase the amount of content aimed at entertaining its primary audience of gay men. Figures 4.3 and 4.4 show that over the first two years of its existence, the channel's programming has moved further away from its description of itself as a serious cultural channel for everyone, heterosexual or homosexual, male or female.[74]

The percentage of serious programming, defined as news, documentaries and debate shows, operas, classical music concerts, theater, and reports on literature and other high-cultural art forms, has declined during the channel's first two years.

The station has also provided less and less programming for its nonhomosexual viewers over this time period. In the chart below (Figure 4.4), the category of "programming for everyone" includes the amount of time devoted to programs whose intended viewers' gender and sexual identities were indeterminate or irrelevant, along

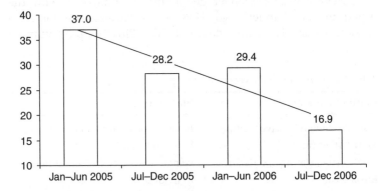

*Figure 4.3*   Percentage of serious programming on PinkTV[a]

Note:[a] The straight line on the chart is a linear trend line.

Information on the methodology for Figures 4.3, 4.4, 4.5, and 4.6 is in endnote 74, p. 146.

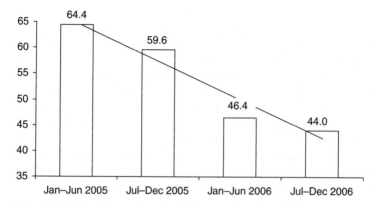

*Figure 4.4* Percentage of programming for everyone on PinkTV[a]
*Note:* [a] The straight line on the chart is a linear trend line.

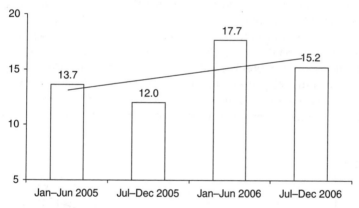

*Figure 4.5* Percentage of programming for lesbians on PinkTV[a]
*Note:* [a] The category of lesbian programming includes all programming made explicitly for lesbians as well as one half of all programming made for the GLBT community in general. The straight line on the chart is a linear trend line.

with one half of the time dedicated to programs dealing with gay icons, drag queens, gay camp, or kitsch, since this last category of programs is less clearly intended for gay viewers exclusively.

It does seem, however, that the amount of programming for lesbians has been increasing slightly (Figure 4.5).

Yet the chart does not take into account the decrease in the amount of time devoted to nonhomosexual viewers, which has led to an increase in programming for both lesbians and gay men. A potentially more useful indicator of PinkTV's commitment to its lesbian audience is the *ratio* of gay male to lesbian programming over time. In the beginning of 2005, for example, there were 1.4 minutes of programming for gay men for every one minute of programming for lesbians. By the end of 2006, however, this ratio had increased to 2.5 minutes of gay male programming for every one minute of lesbian programming. Figure 4.6 shows the ratio of the number of minutes devoted to programming for gay men divided by the number of minutes devoted to programming for lesbians over time.

The charts above give information about the station's programming content, but how can one know anything about the composition of PinkTV's audience? One way is to look at information publicly released by the station. For example, in a press release in September 2005, PinkTV stated that its audience is "primarily male, young, urban and educated," 80 percent male, and 77 percent between the ages of 25 and 44.[75] In its information for potential advertisers, PinkTV describes its audience as 85,000 households made up of "urbanites, professionals, trend setters, technophiles, and hedonists."[76] In addition, Houzelot has estimated that 20 percent of PinkTV's viewers are not gay.[77] Of course, the problem with this kind of information is that it lacks objectivity. These statements may be influenced by what PinkTV wants people,

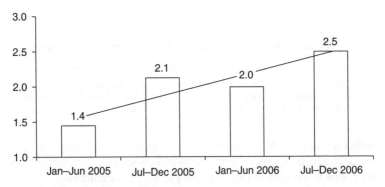

*Figure 4.6*   Ratio of gay male/lesbian programming on PinkTV[a]
Note: The straight line on the chart is a linear trend line.

including potential viewers and advertisers, to believe about their audience, and may not reflect what they actually believe the composition of their audience to be. For example, the estimate of 20 percent nongay viewers seems high, especially since viewers must take the first step of subscribing to the channel and paying the unusually high monthly subscription price of 9 euros (this is quite different from a channel that a heterosexual viewer might stumble upon while channel-surfing). Since it is impossible to determine the sexual orientation of the station's viewers, one must rely on other information.

Advertising for the channel is one possible source of information for determining who PinkTV considers its intended audience to be. Before the channel's launch in 2004, a series of five advertisements appeared on billboards and in magazines. One included the image of two men lying next to one another; another the image of two women lying next to one another; a third was a picture of two men and one woman in a triple embrace; a fourth was of a man and a woman kissing in the front seat of a car; and the fifth was the image of a solitary male standing shirtless under a showerhead. Though the advertisements appear to address a variety of sexual identities, upon closer viewing it seems that the imagery was designed primarily to titillate gay men. In every image except for the one of the two women, there is much more male flesh exposed than female flesh. In the picture of the ostensibly heterosexual couple in the car, for example, the woman is fully dressed, while the man's naked torso occupies virtually the entire image. Similarly, in the picture of the threesome, the woman is almost completely hidden by the naked flesh of the two male bodies. While there are certainly erotic elements in these images that could interest lesbians, heterosexual women, and even heterosexual men, it does not seem that the advertising team was considering these populations to be its primary targets.

Another way to learn more about what PinkTV considers to be its core audience is by examining the content of its flagship program, *Le Set*. It is a useful tool for getting into the heads of the people at PinkTV, not only because it is one of the few programs actually produced by the station, but also because it is among its most popular. According to Pierre Garnier, PinkTV's marketing director, "[t]he programming that works the best is *Le Set* and the cinema selection on Sunday evenings."[78]

It is obvious that *Le Set*'s hosts and the "Pinksetters" (recurring guest-commentators on the show) know that their viewers are almost exclusively gay men. Though they generally make an effort to maintain PinkTV's discourse of inclusiveness, there are moments when they make verbal slips that indicate what they actually think of the audience's composition. An analysis of one month of *Le Set* episodes in April 2006 provided the following examples of such slips: (1) A report on homosexuality in Argentina explained that gay and lesbian tourists are flocking to Buenos Aires where homosexuality is widely accepted. Though the report was allegedly supposed to be for both men and women, the focus was on the reputation of Argentinean men as particularly good-looking, a notion that was confirmed by short interviews with male French tourists.[79] (2) Brigitte Boréale, a Pinksetter, made a report on a gay and lesbian tennis tournament; however, not a single woman was shown in the five interviews with players and the numerous shots of them in action.[80] (3) Beaugrand was a bit overzealous in his desire to maintain the station's rhetoric of inclusiveness when he introduced a report on the Long Yang Club of Paris as an association for "dykes and fags" even though the club is not for women.[81] Similarly in interviews, the hosts have sometimes made errors that provide short glimpses into what they truly think. When asked whether *Le Set* could have been shown on a station for "general audiences," Beaugrand did not correct the interviewer for suggesting that PinkTV was somehow not a station for everyone, but replied, "[i]t might have been a good thing, but I don't know if it would have worked."[82] Similarly, when asked if the show has any taboos, Beaugrand forgets that the show is supposed to be for both heterosexuals and homosexuals when he replies that one example of how there are no taboos "is that we often say 'fag' on the set, but that makes sense, since our show is made for an audience of fags and dykes."[83]

The complicit acceptance of male dominance by the show's hosts and guests is another indication that they believe their audience is made up mostly of gay men. In every episode of *Le Set* for the month of April 2006, for example, Beaugrand managed to get in the last word, often adding a short interjection such as "we love you!" even when it was clear that Labory was the one scripted to speak last. A general appreciation for jocular humor and a prevailing attitude of "boys will be boys" tend to point in the same direction – the show's hosts and guests know that their audience is made up mostly of gay men. In one interview, Beaugrand teasingly referred to Labory in an interview as a "crabby old dyke";[84] an attitude that seems to be confirmed by the following occurrences on the show in April 2006:

- Benjamin Légier, a Pinksetter, demonstrated a new massage chair. He asked Beaugrand to test it out. The two touched each other flirtatiously and made jokes while he tried the chair. Labory and the female guests watched silently while the two gay men had fun. Légier then tested a hand-held massager on the male guests. The men were all laughing while the women remained polite, silent, and stationary. At the end of the show, Beaugrand approached Labory with the hand massager. When he touched her with it, she screamed and pushed him away. She was clearly unhappy, the uptight party pooper, putting an end to the boys' fun.[85]
- Brigitte Boréale, a Pinksetter, reported on the Pagan origins of Easter. Boréale asked Christophe to assist her with the demonstration of an Easter game that involved kicking treats out to the audience. Labory said "Christophe, no, I don't want you to…" Beaugrand kicked one in Labory's direction and it hit her in the chest. The camera turned to Labory's annoyed face and the new chocolate stain on her blouse. While Beaugrand was laughing off-camera, Labory said, "Ok, very well, let's move on."[86]
- Légier talked about downloadable paper costumes for the penis. When he said that they are made for fairly large penises, Légier and Beaugrand started laughing and it was clear that the conversation was only for the gay men. Labory sat silently with her arms crossed.[87]
- Annabelle Troussier, a Pinksetter, reported on antisnoring strips that are placed on the tongue. Troussier: "The little strip is put on the tip of the, of the… on the tongue." Beaugrand [*laughing*]: "On the tip of the… yes?" Troussier [*trying to continue with her report*]: "No, no… it dissolves and the idea is that… it lubricates." Beaugrand [*breaking into laughter again*]: "So is it only for snoring or are there other uses?" Annabelle [*trying to continue*]: "So if you are a well-informed snorer…" (in French, "*un ronfleur averti*"). Beaugrand [*interrupting*]: "An invert snorer?" (in French, "*un ronfleur inverti*"). Annabelle tried to continue with her report by discussing surgical options, including a procedure that increases the diameter of the throat. Beaugrand: "Ah, now you are starting to get interesting! But can you still keep taking the little snoring strips just for

lubrication, once the diameter is enormous?" [*laughter and applause from the audience*].[88]

- While Labory was trying to say what was on the channel later that night, Beaugrand is heard off-camera talking to the guest Thierry Fontez about being single versus in a couple. Beaugrand [*off-camera*]: "Oh it's hard." Fontez: "Always better that way!" Beaugrand [*laughing*]: "Ah that's a good one!" Labory (*annoyed*) "I didn't hear that." Beaugrand [*still laughing*]: "He said that it's better to be hard. Oh whatever."

Moreover, despite the presence of a variety of gender and sexual identities on the show, the nongay male figures tend to have less importance and serve primarily as tokens. Normally "tokenism" refers to the practice of limited inclusion of members of a minority group in order to give the appearance of inclusiveness. In the case of PinkTV, the tokens may include representatives of the minority group of lesbians, although they more frequently come from the dominant population of heterosexuals.

The choice of guests on the *Le Set* has been fairly balanced with approximately 60 percent males and 40 percent females.[89] However, this does not mean that the show is of equal interest to gay men and lesbians. While there is an almost equal number of heterosexual and homosexual male guests, virtually all of the women guests are heterosexual, many of whom are icons for gay men.[90] Similarly for the Pinksetters, 83 percent of the appearances were men (in or out of drag) and 17 percent were women. However, these numbers mask the fact that regardless of the gender of the person presenting information, only 2.2 percent of the reports concerned women viewers specifically, compared to 23.9 percent for men (the remaining 73.9 percent of reports were gender-neutral in terms of their targeted audience).[91]

Virtually all the women who were on the show in April 2006 were heterosexuals, there for the benefit of gay male viewers. For example, Julia Migenes, an opera singer and gay icon, flattered the gay male audience when she explained, "I can do things with a gay male friend that I can't really do with a straight man." Beaugrand asked Migenes whether gay men have been important in her professional life and she answered with a string of compliments for the gay male viewers: "Oh yes. You find them all over in the music and art worlds. They are sensitive. That is, full of creativity and inspiration. It's interesting how many artistic people are gay men."[92] On another episode, Jeane Manson, an American singer and actress, explained her love for gay men in a similar way: "I have lots of gay male friends. I really love them. They have a sensitivity that straight men don't."[93]

Tokens are treated differently from the other people on the show, with their difference tending to be exoticized or derided. For the entire month of April 2006, for example, there was only one case of a woman presenting something for women, and the subject was ridiculed. On that day, Annabelle Troussier, a Pinksetter who reports on medical and health issues, came to discuss the G-spot. She brought a diagram of the female sexual organs and asked Beaugrand to approach the chart so that she could explain it to him. The audience and all the guests erupted into laughter when Beaugrand asked whether she was certain that the chart was not upside-down. He continued to act confused as he pointed to the vagina and asked whether it was the rectum. The audience and guests continued to laugh as he pointed once again and asked "[w]hat's the blue thing? The clitoris? Is a clitoris actually blue?"[94]

On another episode, the coeditors of the gay magazine *Têtu,* Yannick Barbe and Myrtille Rambion, were guests. They came to talk about *Têtue,* the section in *Têtu* dedicated to lesbian readers. Though this part of the show was presumably for lesbians, Labory and the female guests said virtually nothing. It was mainly a plea to the gay male viewers to give *Têtu's* lesbian section a chance. At the end of the show, Barbe provided a description of lesbian humor and what emerged was an image of the lesbian as an exotic, unfamiliar creature: "For some time now, with the arrival of *Têtue,* a section that is 100% lesbian, a lesbian humor has begun to emerge. That is... I don't want to say that before lesbians were humorless... Lesbian humor... I recommend it to you, in fact, I recommend it to all the boys. ... I can tell you that when we have an office meeting at *Têtu,* the girls are there. And I can tell you that the most hilarious and crazy subjects come from the girls, and that makes me happy."[95]

### There's nothing queer about PinkTV

Since its creation in 2004, PinkTV has striven to align its description of itself with the ideals of French Republicanism by asserting that it is a serious cultural channel for everyone, gay or straight, male or female. Beginning with the fall 2006 season, however, the channel seems to have begun the process of coming out as an openly gay station with programming that is more explicitly designed to entertain its core audience. In every press release issued since the station began, the PinkTV has described itself as a generalist channel, that is, for all audiences. However, in the press release from October 2006, the adjective "generalist" was suddenly nowhere to be found and the most recent statements from the station indicate that it is realigning its description of itself to match the evolution in the character of its programming more closely. In the end, these most recent descriptions of the channel indicate that though it still might not be easy to come out as a gay media form in France, it is perhaps becoming a bit easier.

> [The new season is] primarily about recalibrating the three editorial axes of the channel: *Entertainment,* because PinkTV is and will remain more than anything a channel for entertainment – *Proximity,* our channel should reflect the lives and the day-to-day of our subscribers – Culture, but *culture that is accessible and unifying.*[96]

Despite this recent recognition by PinkTV's directors that the station is there primarily to entertain, to provide accessible culture, and to serve its gay audience, expressed somewhat hesitantly with the word "proximity," the channel has only cautiously begun to open the closet's door. In a special television debate on the issue of coming out, Alex Taylor the host of the show asked "a final question about PinkTV itself. Is it important for the channel... to come out of the closet as gay?" At this point, the sociologist Marie-Hélène Bourcier reminded him that "even today, certain closets remain. There are things people just don't see: a more normal version [of homosexuality], that is always better-looking, nicer. Today we heard guests say 'no [transvestites with] high heels,' 'no sadomasochism'; things still cannot go beyond certain limits."[97]

Even though PinkTV describes itself as a channel for all sexualities and genders, there is nothing queer – in the sense of a call to arms against identities built around fixed, binary notions of gender and sexuality – about the station's programming. Instead, PinkTV's presentation of a spectrum of sexual and gender identities is primarily a form of tokenism. To the degree that tokenism does nothing to blur categories of gender and sexuality but in fact serves to reify them, the station's contents represent something quite different from an assertion of queer identity. Generally, tokenism is assumed to be an essentially American practice stemming from communitarian identity politics, but it is also possible to imagine a distinctly French form of it. American-style tokenism normally involves including members of a minority group in spaces traditionally occupied by the dominant majority in an effort to appear inclusive. However, the French brand of tokenism seen on PinkTV does the opposite: it includes representatives of the dominant majority in a space intended for members of a minority group in order to avoid being accused of self-ghettoization. PinkTV's use of a broad range of gender and sexual identities is not about blurring gender and sexual categories, but stems from the need for the channel to present itself as embracing French universalism and as refusing to cater to a single minority group. In the end, the creation of PinkTV, like other manifestations of "gay pride" in France, does not seriously call into question the French republican model of universalism. The station's descriptions of itself, and in particular its need to distance itself from the label *"communautaire,"* in fact confirms the continued rhetorical force of republicanism in France.

# Conclusion: QUEER, *Made in France*[1]

In writing about the situation of homosexuals in other countries, we Americans are sometimes tempted to speak in terms of their retarded development. However, in comparing the progress of American and French gay political groups during the last 25 years, it becomes difficult to see in what ways French political activists have fallen behind relative to their American counterparts. Republican assimilationist strategies have served French homosexuals well, being responsible for an impressive series of legal reforms, particularly in contrast to what has happened in the United States during the same time. France has removed all explicit legal discrimination against homosexuals, while the United States' military policy of "don't ask, don't tell" continues to explicitly discriminate against gays and lesbians, and consensual sexual acts conducted in private between same-sex individuals were a crime in many American states until the recent Supreme Court decision in *Lawrence and Garner* v. *Texas*.[2] In 1985, France passed legislation protecting individuals from discrimination based on their sexual orientation, whereas most American gays and lesbians still do not benefit from such protection: none exists at the federal level and the scope of the various cities' and states' antidiscrimination laws is limited. Finally, France has made a legally recognized partnership structure available to French same-sex couples. While civil unions in Vermont, Connecticut, and New Jersey and same-sex marriages in Massachusetts and California provide limited benefits, many states along with the federal government have passed "defense of marriage" acts, which explicitly define marriage as between a man and a woman. All these examples challenge the notion that, compared to the United States, France is simply caught in a more primitive stage of political evolution and that by stub-bornly remaining "in the closet," contemporary French gay people have not lived up to their American counterparts' example. The recent history of French gay politics is a reminder that in foreign places, other logics produce different, yet equally legitimate, strat-egies adapted to the constraints of their particular environments.

In this conclusion, I would like to turn away from the past and look toward the future to speculate on the effects of the recent arrival of American queer theory in France. What kind of use will be made of these ideas given the continued force of universalist, republican rhet-oric in France? And what effect will the reception of these subversive ideas in France have on the future of French Republicanism? Before considering what a linguistic and cultural translation of the American term "queer" into the context of contemporary France might look like, it is first necessary to stabilize the term's shifting meaning in the American context. American debates over the meaning of "queer" are frequent and sometimes ferocious, but there is some common ground for its use: it refers to a flexible identity that is constantly in motion, constantly becoming, constantly transgressing. The ques-tion then becomes, how to go about fixing the meaning of a term that challenges the fixity of meaning itself? For the purposes of this analysis, it seems possible to isolate at least two defining characteris-tics in the use of the term "queer" in the common ground of Anglo American debates. First, to be queer is to be against assimilationism. In the early days of the queer movement, the term "queer" explicitly asserted an "in-your-face difference with an edge of defiant separat-ism: 'We're here, we're queer, get used to it,' [went] the chant. We are different, that is, free from convention, odd and out there and proud of it."[3] In recent years, however, antiassimilationism has become so self-evident to groups such as Queer Nation that it is perhaps no longer necessary to state it explicitly in contemporary assertions of the meaning of "queer." With time, the use of "queer" has moved beyond simple antiassimilationism toward a more destabilizing rebellion against the formation of identities around fixed poles of gender or sexuality. This call to arms against fixed, binary identities is the second prong of my working definition.

Contemporary queers claim to have opened a new theoretical space: a space in which desire, the body, and sexuality have become primary. In this new space, desire is not only considered primary, but autonomous. As an autonomous force, desire cannot be understood as socially or historically determined. For Anglo American queers, the goal is to defy the social and historical construction of categories of sexuality and gender, and in particular, the fixed identities of straight, gay, lesbian, and bisexual, because any construction of identity only serves to restrict the autonomous expression or performance of desire. Of course, this act of defiance presupposes the existence of sexual identities. To defy the limits of straight, gay, lesbian, or bisexual identities, the identities must be understood to exist. This notion poses particular problems when translated into a French context, since as we have already seen, the a priori existence of sexual categories in France is far from axiomatic.

In June 1997, the Centre Pompidou hosted the first conference on queer theory in France. When the presentations were done and the discussion was opened to the floor, I was surprised by the hostile tone of many of the questions and reactions from the audience. The hostility manifested itself in different forms, from the ugliness of the word "queer" and its strange pronunciation in French, to the inappropriateness of these American ideas within the French social model, since for many French gays and lesbians, rhetoric perceived as stemming from American-style identity politics is met with skepticism. The French sociologist Frédéric Martel warns, for example, that French gay activists "who attempt to imitate the American model, unless they are prepared to completely dismantle the French model of integrating individuals, need to realize that such surgical operations could prove perilous in a country where no tradition of communitarianism exists, at least not yet."[4]

Since the original conference at the Centre Pompidou, some French theorists have taken a new and hesitant look at queer theory, and in recent years, France has witnessed the development of a small but vocal queer movement "made in France." An organization calling itself *Le Zoo* has organized a series of seminars to address the question of how one might go about importing American queer theory into the French context. In 1998, they published a collection of articles on this question in a book entitled *Q comme Queer*. In the preface, Catherine Deschamps, a founding member of *Le Zoo*, provides a possible definition of "queer" for a French audience:

> Queer is non-assimilationist and non-essentialist. There, that's all
> I have to say. We don't feel like making some kind of pedagogical

spectacle on what queer is anyway – to understand what queer is in the United States would lead us into a long debate. As for what it could be in France...we have quite a bit to say. Mostly because the French social and historical context is different from the American context and in France, the notion of queer collides with the sacrosanct principle of integration *à la française*.[5]

Already we see here a desire to liberate the French use of "queer" from the American usage and an attempt to start breaking down the particular limitations of French assimilationism. The point is not to defy preexisting identities, but to establish a distinct new identity; one that is constructed in opposition to French bourgeois heteronormativity, as explained by self-proclaimed French queer activist, Marie-Hélène Bourcier: "Our presuppositions are the opposite of those of the assimilationists: we are different and our difference allows us to resist discourse, practices and laws which do not want us to be different."[6] Here, we see the primacy of antias- similationism in this French understanding of "queer," one that seems to recognize rather explicitly the impossibility of a direct importation of American queer theory and its calls for the blurring of categories of identity. Bourcier's concluding remarks in *Q comme Queer* bring this out most clearly: "In the United States...one of the reasons for the existence of queer over there is to undo these iden- tities which threaten to become natural. In France, however, the idea of 'queer' can first serve to build up an identity in the classic sense."[7]

Since the publication of *Q comme Queer* in 1998, queer theory has received increased attention in France, and the understanding of queer theory has gone beyond mere antiassimilationism to include the blurring and defiance of binary categories of identity, or the second prong of my working definition of "queer." In 2003, *Rue Descartes*, published a volume, *Queer: repenser les identités* that made it clear that a lot had changed in France since 1998. Part of this is certainly due to the fact that a number of English-language books, including Eve Sedgwick's *Epistemology of the Closet* and Judith Butler's *Gender Trouble* along with works by David Halperin, Jonathan Katz, Vernon Rosario, and Leo Bersani have recently been translated into French. Still, the contributors to *Queer: repenser les identités* con- tinued to find a number of problems with a direct importation of American-style queer theory.

The most important criticisms of queer theory in France stem from the fact that it originated in the United States. Resistance to queer represents for some, a resistance to American imperialism: "the transplantation [of queer theory] goes in the classical direction of American cultural hegemony toward countries subjected to this hegemony.... For it is well known that the United States exports its dominant culture with as much ardor as it exports its subcultures."[8] Another problem is that the English word "queer" has no history in France: Can queer mean the same thing if it only exists as a translation? How can one "take on this emerging thought without knowing what preceded it, what it is in dialogue with, and what new things it proposes? In order to discuss queer theory, it's first necessary to construct an infrastructure."[9] Perhaps then it is necessary to invent another French word for these ideas, "a word that the [local] homosexual community has already suffered from. Once it's transplanted, the status of the word changes. Its ability to strike hard, to effect change, is lost in the [trans-Atlantic] journey."[10]

The risk is that the word "queer" could become an "empty-signifier" in France, leaving its definition open to anyone and allowing its meaning to be distorted for almost any strategic purpose. Some have argued that this has already happened in France with interpretations of Foucault, whose writings have been used in a variety of strange ways, including as justification for gay people to live "with discretion." Contributors to *Queer: repenser les identités* explain that queer terminology "runs the risk of carrying some 'snob value' or at best of being part of a 'cult theory' more than that of a catalyzing political idea." As is often the case with the importation of foreign terms, there is a risk of creating a special clique of people who are "in the know" and can throw around terms like *"performatif"* and other terms of art. Such a use of queer theory obviously runs counter to its original political intent.

Some French defenders of queer theory have avoided the issue of American cultural imperialism by arguing that even if the ideas originated in the United States, the concepts themselves are essentially anti-American. Beatriz Preciado argues that national borders no longer matter for queer theory. It benefits from globalization and is a form of cultural production that defies national or linguistic borders. She suggests that it is a mistake to call it an American movement, since it is fundamentally a criticism of American imperialism.

"Queer theory provokes an incessant transgression (in the geographic sense of the term) of borders, which is not irrelevant at a time when we're witnessing the decomposition of traditional nation-states and an outbreak of nationalist politics. This crisis of the national body is mirrored by the crisis of the modern sexual body."[11] She argues that globalization is in fact a double-edged sword. On the one hand, it means the decline of nation-states' sovereignty, but it also allows for the emergence of transnational social movements, such as ACT-UP, Amnesty International, Queer Watch, and Queers for Racial and Economic Justice, as political actors, groups that unite ethnic and sexual minorities and give them a voice.

Perhaps paradoxically, another type of criticism of queer theory is not that it is American, but that it is French. This critique argues that there's nothing original or radical about queer theory, which is a mere outgrowth of 1970s French thought, and a watered-down version of French thinkers like Foucault, at that. Queer theory is seen as a pale imitation of these theorists, lacking their rigor and subtlety. Still others have argued that there are more important things to think about than gender and sexuality, such as the spread of free market globalization and the rise of nationalism in Europe.

In the end, it is clear that whatever "queer" comes to mean in France, it will have a distinctly French flavor. As Denis Provencher has recently pointed out, though French gays and lesbians may appear somewhat proficient in Anglo American queer rhetoric, "they still frame their conversations largely in relation to local historical, cultural, and literary specificities informed by a French republican language of integration and a queer French language tradition of non-identitarian desire."[12] Similarly, in his analysis of the alleged "Americanization" of French gay and lesbian movements, William Poulin-Deltour explains that "while there may be agreement that American *forms*, such as 'community centers,' have crossed the Atlantic, the *content* or *filling* of these forms varies widely between French and American contexts."[13] He adds that changes associated with the American model, "do not simply sweep away French social and cultural characteristics. Rather, they are appropriated, structured and deployed in relation to those characteristics, thereby reproducing national differences between France and the United States."[14] One thing that is certain is that unlike Anglo American articulations of queer, "queer *made in France*" will be responding to French republicanism in one way or another – and if the recent history of gay political strategies serves as an example, the Republic will be elastic enough to accommodate the subversive aspects of these new ideas.

Indeed, there are indications that accommodation could happen quite easily; especially if one imagines that France is already "queer" in some, perhaps unintentional way, in a distinctly French way that does not require political mobilization around communitarian sexual identities. According to the porn director, Bruce LaBruce, this might just be the case: "France seems particularly queer to me. France has always had a certain *je ne sais quoi* that announces to the rest of the world that it is queer. It's something they all share, a meticulous attention to detail, an appreciation of the better things in life."[15] It is perhaps a bit of a caricature, but the French are often thought of in the following queer ways: as people who recognize the primacy of desire and pleasure; who are reluctant to build social identities around sexual practices; who value the absurd, the irrational, the superficial, and the frivolous – in short, a culture that understands and appreciates the performative aspects of social behavior. Could it mean that inadvertently, the elastic closet of French republicanism already has at its disposal the means to accommodate this latest attempt at subversion?

# Notes

## Introduction: Republican Values and the Depenalization of Sodomy in France

1. Unless otherwise noted, all translations in this book from French to English are those of the author.
2. Joseph-Marie Hulewicz, "Réflexion: La phobie de l'homosexualité," *Gai pied hebdo*, 29 October 1992, 13.
3. For a discussion of literary and artistic representations of lesbians in the nineteenth century, see Gretchen Schultz, "La Rage du plaisir et la rage de la douleur: Lesbian Pleasure and Suffering in Fin-de-siècle French Literature and Sexology," in *Pleasure and Pain*, eds. David Evans and Kate Griffiths (Amsterdam: Rodopi, 2009); Leslie Choquette, "Homosexuals in the City: Representations of Lesbian and Gay Space in Nineteenth-Century Paris," *Journal of Homosexuality* 41, no. 3/4 (2001), 149–68; and Victoria Thompson, "Creating Boundaries: Homosexuality and the Changing Social Order in France, 1830–1870," in *Homosexuality in Modern France*, eds. Jeffrey Merrick and Bryant T. Ragan, Jr. (New York: Oxford University Press, 1996), 102–27.
4. The age of sexual majority for heterosexuals was 13 in 1942. In 1945, the ages of sexual majority were set at 15 for heterosexuals and 21 for homosexuals. In 1974, the ages were changed once again to 15 for heterosexuals and 18 for homosexuals.
5. Law of 25 September–6 October 1791. A few other European countries, such as the Netherlands in 1811, would eventually adopt the French penal code after having it brought to them by French revolutionary and imperial armies (see Theo Van der Meer, "Sodomy and the Pursuit of a Third Sex in the Early Modern Period," in *Third Sex/Third Gender: Beyond Sexual Dimorphism in Culture and History*, ed. Gilbert Herdt [New York: Zone Books, 1994], 141–2).
6. Daniel Borillo, "Statut juridique de l'homosexualité et droits de l'homme," *Cahiers Gai Kitsch Camp*, ed. Rommel Medès-Leite, no. 28: "Un sujet inclassable? Approches sociologiques, littéraires et juridiques des homosexualités," Lille, February 1995, 100. See also Gonfroys, F., *Un fait de civilisation méconnu: l'homosexualité à Rome* (Poitiers: Thèse, 1972), and especially, Paul Veyne, "Homosexuality in Ancient Rome," in *Western Sexuality: Practice and Precept in Past and Present*, eds. Philippe Ariès and André Béjin (Oxford: Blackwell, 1985); originally in *Sexualités Occidentales, Communications* (Paris: Seuil, 1982), 26–35.
7. Codex Theod. IX, 7, 3, in Maurice Lever, *Les bûchers de Sodome* (Paris: Favard, 1985), 34.
8. Lever, *Les bûchers de Sodome*, 37.
9. Lever, *Les bûchers de Sodome*, 51.

10. For the purposes of these sections, the term "sodomy" is used to refer to homosexual acts between consenting adults.

11. Lever, *Les bûchers de Sodome*, 51.

12. Throughout this chapter and those following, the term "homosexual" will be the most general term for any person practicing same-sex sexual acts regardless of the historical context. Other terms, such as "sodomite," "invert," *"pederast,"* "homophile," and "gay" will be used to denote homosexuals in specific historical moments with an emphasis on the terms' historical contexts.

13. Lever, *Les bûchers de Sodome*, 50–1.

14. William Peniston, "A Public Offense against Decency: the Trial of the Count de Germiny and the 'Moral Order' of the Third Republic," *Disorder in the Court: Trials and Sexual Conflict at the Turn of the Century*, eds. George Robb and Nancy Erber (New York: New York UP, 1999), 12.

15. Michael David Sibalis, "The Regulation of Male Homosexuality in Revolutionary and Napoleonic France, 1789–1815," in *Homosexuality in Modern France*, eds. Jeffrey Merrick and Bryant T. Ragan, Jr., 82.

16. William A. Peniston, *Pederasts and Others: Urban Culture and Sexual Identity in Nineteenth-Century Paris* (New York: Harrington Park Press, 2004), 15.

17. Sibalis, "Regulation of Male Homosexuality," 82 (emphasis added).

18. Ibid.

19. Bryant T. Ragan, Jr., "The Enlightenment Confronts Homosexuality," in *Homosexuality in Modern France*, eds. Jeffrey Merrick and Bryant T. Ragan, Jr., 25.

20. Sibalis, "Regulation of Male Homosexuality," 82.

21. Ibid.

22. Emile Garçon, *Code pénal annoté: Nouvelle edition refondue et mise à jour*, 3 vols (Paris, 1952–1959) 3, 194, cited in Sibalis, "Regulation of Male Homosexuality," 82. It is of course questionable whether rape should be classified as a "sex crime" as opposed to a crime of violence.

23. Law of 19–22 July 1791, Chapter II, Article 8, cited in Sibalis, "Regulation of Male Homosexuality," 83.

24. Michael Sibalis, "Jean-Jacques-Régis Cambacérès," in *Who's Who in Contemporary Gay & Lesbian History: From Antiquity to World War II*, eds. Robert Aldrich and Garry Wotherspoon (London: Routledge, 2001), 80.

25. Ibid.

26. AN, D III 266, Copie des jugements rendus par le Tribunal de la police correctionnelle, 28 Pluviôse and 28 Ventôse Year II (16 February and 18 March 1794), Jugement rendu par le Tribunal d'appel de la police du Département de Paris, 8 Germinal Year II (28 March 1794), cited in Sibalis, "Regulation of Male Homosexuality," 83–4.

27. Sibalis, "Regulation of Male Homosexuality," 83–4.

28. Observations des tribunaux criminels sur le projet de code criminel, 6 vols (Paris, an XIII), III, section "Indre," 6, cited in Sibalis, "Regulation of Male Homosexuality," 98.

29. Bibliothèque Nationale, Ms N.A.Fr. 3533, folio 351–2, report by Piquenard to the President of the Executive Directory, 5 Prairial AN VI (24 May 1798), cited in Maurice Lever, *Les bûchers de Sodome*, 398–9.

30. Sibalis, "Regulation of Male Homosexuality," 90–1. Documents from the trial are available in AN, BB18 309, dossier C-4610, Poullin to Guillard, 30 Floréal Year XIII (20 May 1805).

31. Ibid.

32. AN, BB2 3, "Feuille du travail du ministre de la Justice avec Sa Majesté l'empereur, 28 messidor an XIII (17 July 1805)," no. 36, cited in Sibalis, "Regulation of Male Homosexuality," 91–2.

33. Adolphe Cheveau and Faustin Hélie, *Théorie du Code pénal*, 8 vols. (Paris: 1837–1842) 6:110–12, cited in Sibalis, "Regulation of Male Homosexuality," 85.

34. Marc Daniel, "Histoire de la législation pénale concernant l'homosexualité," *Arcadie*, January 1962, 14.

35. Jean Danet, "Discours juridique et perversions sexuelles (XIXe et XXe siècles)," *Famille et Politique* 6, Centre de recherche politique de l'Université de Nantes (1997), 11.

36. Jean-Etienne-Marie Portalis, *L'âme universelle de la legislation,* cited in François Ewald and Pierre Antoine Fenet, eds., *Naissance du Code Civil* (Paris: Flammarion, 1989), 276.

37. Referring to the United States here is somewhat misleading, since sodomy was a crime in individual American states (as opposed to a federal crime). In the section following, references to the United States are actually referring to those specific jurisdictions that have had sodomy laws.

38. Portalis, *Discours Préliminaire*, cited in Ewald and Fenet, 38.

39. *Model Penal Code* § 213.2, Comment 2 (1962, comments revised 1980), cited in William B. Rubenstein, *Lesbians, Gay Men, and the Law* (New York: The New Press, 1993), 88.

40. *Bowers* was overturned in 2003 by *Lawrence and Garner v. Texas*, 539 U.S. 558 (2003).

41. *Bowers v. Hardwick*, 478 U.S. 186 (1986).

42. *Bowers v. Hardwick*, Chief Justice Burger, concurring.

43. Danet, "Discours juridique," 10–11.

44. Régis Revenin, *Homosexualité et prostitution masculines à Paris: 1870–1918* (Paris: L'Harmattan, 2005), 156.

45. Félix Carlier, *Les Deux prostitutions* (Paris: Dentu, 1887), cited in Pierre Hahn, *Nos ancêtres les pervers: La vie des homosexuels sous le Second Empire* (Paris: Olivier Orban, 1979), 446.

46. Carlier, *Les Deux prostitutions*, cited in Pierre Hahn, *Nos ancêtres les pervers*, 287.

47. For example, a typical excerpt from one letter reads: "these people get together at 8, rue Crussol, at Mr. Lamontagne's house" ("Pédérastes, 1820–1882" [A.P.P. DA 230 (6)], 428 pieces, 1st division, 2nd bureau, Document no. 423, Archives de la Préfecture de Police de Paris).

48. "Pédérastes, 1820–1882," Document no. 413.

49. The arrest report appears in "Pédérastes, 1820–1882," Document no. 411.
50. Peniston, *Pederasts and Others*, 11.
51. Leslie Choquette, "Homosexuals in the City: Representations of Lesbian and Gay Space in Nineteenth-Century Paris," *Journal of Homosexuality* 41, no. 3/4 (2001): 162.
52. Peniston, *Pederasts and Others*, 142.
53. Revenin, 17–65.
54. Steven Green, *Foucault's Panopticon,* January 1999, *The Theory Site*, 25 July, 1999, http://www.leeds.ac.uk/ics/ctr-fou3.htm.
55. "Pédérastes, 1820–1882," Document no. 310 through 337, Carton 230.
56. "Pédérastes, 1820–1882," Document no. 336, Carton 230.
57. Carlier, in his memoirs, dedicated a special section to the case of homosexual members of the military: "But the soldier, who can be judged by any of his hierarchical superiors, not just those from his regiment, but any of those he might meet regardless of the regiment to which they belong, does not have full freedom to behave as he wishes. He cannot, without exposing himself to serious punishment, let down his guard in the street or in a public establishment, as a civilian could do. Military discipline requires of him great discretion, which he cannot abandon without danger. He, therefore, needs special sites, meeting places sheltered from the risk of inopportune meetings or indiscreet glances. All of this has been taken care of. There exist two or three establishments, each with a café on the ground floor and furnished rooms on the floors above. These establishments, which are run by *pédérastes* are especially designed for members of the military" (Carlier, *Les Deux prostitutions*, cited in Pierre Hahn, *Nos ancêtres les pervers*, 137).
58. "Pédérastes, 1820–1882," Document no. 319.
59. "Pédérastes, 1820–1882," Document no. 319.
60. "Pédérastes, 1820–1882," Document no. 328.
61. Carlier explains the role of female prostitutes in these meeting places frequented by homosexual members of the military: "Well, it is necessary for these soldiers to shield themselves from the consequences which their alleged or revealed presence in such a place might have for them; so, two or three female prostitutes, who get free lodging on one of the upper floors of the building, are there to protect appearances. In the event of an investigation, it is always at one of these prostitutes' places that the guilty party claims to have stayed, which the others then all affirm" (Carlier, *Les Deux prostitutions*, cited in Pierre Hahn, *Nos ancêtres les pervers*, 137–8).
62. It is interesting to note the hypermasculine discourse evident in Monsieur Cabanier's oral testimony: "he said that just hearing about such things is enough to make him 'blow his top ... and that he would slice open the face of anyone who would say such things to him" ("Pédérastes, 1820–1882," Document no. 325(I)).
63. It is important to remember that these oral testimonies were never written by the witnesses themselves. They were systematically re-transcribed from the verbal information provided by the witnesses, which is frequently evident in the overly formalized language found in these documents.

64. "Pédérastes, 1820–1882," Document no. 319.
65. Ambroise Tardieu, *Etude sur les attentats aux moeurs*, 6th edition (1873), cited in Pierre Hahn, *Nos ancêtres les pervers*, 193–214, cited in 197, 203.
66. Tardieu, *Etude sur les attentats aux moeurs*, cited in Pierre Hahn, *Nos ancêtres les pervers*, 210.
67. Doctor Paul Garnier, "Rapport médico-légal," *Annales d'hygiène publique et de médecine mentale*, Tome XXXIII, 3rd Series, January–June 1895, cited in Pierre Hahn, *Nos ancêtres les pervers*, 228.
68. Gretchen Schultz, "La Rage du plaisir et la rage de la douleur: Lesbian Pleasure and Suffering in Fin-de-siècle French Literature and Sexology," in *Pleasure and Pain*, eds. David Evans and Kate Griffiths.
69. Carolyn J. Dean, *The Frail Social Body: Pornography, Homosexuality, and Other Fantasies in Interwar France* (Berkeley: University of California Press, 2000), 143–4.
70. Dean, *The Frail Social Body*, 130–73.
71. Dr René Allendy and de Hella Lobstein, *Le Problème sexuel à l'école* (Paris: Aubier, 1938), 54, cited in Florence Tamagne, *Histoire de l'homosexualité en Europe: Berlin, Londres, Paris 1919–1939* (Paris: Seuil, 2000), 345.
72. Tamagne, *Histoire*, 91.
73. *Inversions*, no. 2, cited in Gilles Barbadette and Michel Carassou, *Paris Gay 1925* (Paris: Presses de Renaissance, 1981), 188.
74. *Inversions*, no. 3, cited in Barbadette and Carassou, *Paris Gay 1925*, 209.
75. Tamagne, *Histoire*, 138.

# 1   It Could Have Been Worse (1940s–1960s)

1. Gérard Miller, *Les pousse-au-jouir du Maréchal Pétain* (Paris: Le Seuil, 1975), 47, cited in Danet, "Discours juridique," 10.
2. Law of August 6, 1942, *Journal officiel "Lois et Décrets,"* August 27, 1942, 2922.
3. Julian Jackson, "Sex, Politics and Morality in France, 1954–1982," *History Workshop Journal* 61 (2006), 84.
4. "Attentat aux Moeurs," *Jurisclasseur Pénal*, Articles 330–3, section 164: 21.
5. Technically, the ordinance of July 2, 1945 set the age of sexual majority at fifteen for "everyone." However, its scope was limited to heterosexuals, since sexual acts with a person of the same sex under the age of twenty-one were criminalized by Article 331.
6. Ordinance of February 8, 1945, no. 45–190, *Journal officiel "Lois et Décrets,"* February 9, 1945, 650.
7. Law of July 5, 1974, no. 74–631, article 15, *Journal officiel "Lois et Décrets,"* July 7, 1974, 7099.
8. Danet, "Discours juridique," 78.
9. The Germans had their own term for homosexuality: "The French evil." For more on the association of homosexuality with foreignness see Tamagne, *Histoire*, 354.

10. For a discussion of the scapegoating of homosexuals during the interwar period, see Dean, *The Frail Social Body*, 130–73.
11. AN, CAC, 950395, article 4 (D. 2718), dossier 60-SL: Attentats à la pudeur (1945), May 9, 1939 letter from the members of the jury in the Roger Neuville trial.
12. AN, CAC, 950395, article 4 (D. 2718), dossier 60-SL: Attentats à la pudeur (1945), June 10, 1939 report from Médan, 8.
13. Michael Sibalis, "Homophobia, Vichy France, and the 'Crime of Homosexuality': The Origins Of The Ordinance Of 6 August 1942," *GLQ: A Journal of Lesbian and Gay Studies* 8, 3 (2002), 301–18.
14. Tamagne, *Histoire*, 354.
15. AN, CAC, 950395, article 4 (D. 2718), dossier 60-SL: Attentats à la pudeur (1945), December 22, 1941 report from the deputy public prosecutor of Toulon, 2–3. Strangely enough, the author of this text, Charles Dubost, is better known for his activities in the French resistance. He was recognized for his efforts by being chosen to participate in the French delegation of prosecutors in the Nuremberg trials (Marc Boninchi, *Vichy et l'ordre moral* [Paris: Presses Universitaires de France, 2005], 146).
16. December 22, 1941 report from the deputy public prosecutor of Toulon, 4.
17. Gilles Martinez, "Joseph Barthélémy et la crise de la démocratie libérale," *Vingtième Siècle: Revue d'histoire* 59 (1998) 40, http://www.persee.fr/showPage.do?urn=xxs_0294-1759_1998_num_59_1_3776.
18. AN, CAC, 950395, article 4 (D. 2718), dossier 60-SL: Attentats à la pudeur (1945), April 14, 1942 letter from Admiral François Darlan.
19. Ibid.
20. Ibid.
21. Marc Boninchi, *Vichy et l'ordre moral*, 156.
22. AN, CAC, 950395, article 4 (D. 2718), dossier 60-SL: Attentats à la pudeur (1945), March 13, 1942 Note for the Minister of Justice, 3.
23. Handwritten message on the note of March 13, 1942 for the Minister of Justice, 3. Henri Corvisy was identified as the author of the message by Marc Boninchi (Boninchi, *Vichy et l'ordre moral*, 151).
24. June 10, 1939 report from Médan, 2–3.
25. AN, CAC, 950395, article 4 (D. 2718), dossier 60-SL: Attentats à la pudeur (1945), December 22, 1941 report from the deputy public prosecutor of Toulon, 3.
26. June 10, 1939 report from Médan, 5.
27. December 22, 1941 report from the deputy public prosecutor of Toulon, 3.
28. AN, CAC, 950395, article 4 (D. 2718), dossier 60-SL : Attentats à la pudeur (1945), November 9, 1942 letter from Admiral Auphan.
29. Martinez, "Joseph Barthélémy," 46.
30. Ordinance of February 8, 1945 [emphasis added].
31. *Jurisclasseur,* Correctional Tribunal of the Seine, February 9, 1965.
32. Michèle-Laure Rassat, "Inceste et Droit Pénal," *La Semaine Juridique* (1974): I.2614.
33. Danet, "Discours juridique," 87.

34. This is based on the total number of cases of "Détournement de Mineurs" or "Excitation de Mineurs à la Débauche" in Paris from 1928 to 1953 (the last year for which data were available) recorded in the arrest registers in the Archives de la préfecture de police de Paris. Note that the category "Excitation de Mineurs à la Débauche" changed its name to "Excitation de Mineurs à la Débauche – Homosexualité" beginning in 1950, without any noticeable change in the number of cases after the change.

35. Yves Lamou, "Le Point sur le délit d'outrages publics à la pudeur," *Arcadie*, July–August 1975, 350.

36. Lamou, "Le Point," 353.

37. Michael Sibalis, "Paul Mirguet," in *Who's Who in Contemporary Gay & Lesbian History: From Antiquity to World War II*, eds. Robert Aldrich and Garry Wotherspoon (London: Routledge, 2001), 285.

38. *Journal officiel*, Assemblée Nationale, no. 19, annex no. 733, Projet de loi, July 6, 1960.

39. *Journal officiel*, Assemblée Nationale, no. 26, annex no. 819, Projet de loi, July 21, 1960 [emphasis added].

40. *Journal officiel*, Assemblée Nationale, no. 51 (19 July 1960), 1981.

41. Ibid.

42. "Pédéraste" Binders, no. January 2, 1965, Archives of *Gai pied*.

43. Ordinance of November 25, 1960, no. 60–1245, *Journal officiel "Lois et Décrets,"* November 27, 1960, 10603.

44. Sibalis, "Paul Mirguet," 285.

45. Marc Daniel, "Histoire de la législation pénale française concernant l'homosexualité," *Arcadie*, December 1961, 618.

46. Olivier Jablonski, "The Birth of a French Homosexual Press in the 1950s," trans. Michael Sibalis, *Journal of Homosexuality* 41, no. 3/4 (2001), 235.

47. Jacques Girard, *Le mouvement homosexuel en France 1945–1980* (Paris: Syros, 1981), 35.

48. AP, Audience de la 15e chambre correctionnelle, July 18, 1953, cited in Jablonski, "The Birth of a French Homosexual Press," 236.

49. AP, Audience de la 17e chambre correctionnelle, April 26, 1956, cited in Jablonski, "The Birth of a French Homosexual Press," 236.

50. André Baudry, *Arcadie*, no. 82. A Dutchman, Arent Van Sunthorst, invented the term homophile in 1949. The argument was that the word "homosexual" was inappropriate because "homo" comes from Greek, while "sexual" comes from the Latin (Girard, *Le mouvement homosexuel*, 49).

51. Y.E., "La fin d'*Arcadie*?" *Gai pied*, no. 40 (July 1982), 7.

52. "Des homosexuels sous condition," *Gai pied*, no. 38 (May 1982), 12.

53. Interviews by the author of members of *Les gais retraités*, February–May 1995, Paris, France.

54. André Baudry quoted in Girard, *Le mouvement homosexuel*, 58.

55. "Pédéraste" Binders, no. January 2, 1965, Archives of *Gai pied*.

56. Georges Sidéris, "Folles, Swells, Effeminates, and Homophiles in Saint-Germain-des-Prés of the 1950s: A New 'Precious' Society?'" trans. Michael Sibalis, *Journal of Homosexuality* 41, no. 3/4 (2001), 220.

57. André Baudry quoted in Girard, *Le mouvement homosexuel*, 60.

58. André Baudry quoted in Girard, *Le mouvement homosexuel,* 60.
59. André Baudry, "La pédérastie," *Arcadie,* August–September 1968, 319.
60. Gérard Bach-Ignasse, personal interview by author, Paris, France, May 2, 1997.
61. Jablonski, "The Birth of a French Homosexual Press," 239.
62. Jablonski, "The Birth of a French Homosexual Press," 240.
63. Ibid.
64. Interviews by the author of members of *Les gais retraités,* February–May 1995, Paris, France.
65. To preserve anonymity, the first name used here is false.
66. To preserve anonymity, the first name used here is false.
67. Jablonski, "The Birth of a French Homosexual Press," 240.
68. Jablonski, "The Birth of a French Homosexual Press," 240–1.

## 2 Attempts at Subversion (The 1970s)

1. Girard, *Le mouvement homosexuel,* 81.
2. Jackson, "Sex, Politics and Morality," 87–88.
3. Girard, *Le mouvement homosexuel,* 80.
4. Enda McCaffrey, *The Gay Republic: Sexuality, Citizenship and Subversion in France* (London: Ashgate, 2005), 195.
5. "Prolétaires de tous les pays, caressez-vous!" *Gulliver,* November 1972.
6. Girard, *Le mouvement homosexuel,* 81.
7. Vicky, "Harmonie ou si l'homosexualité m'était contée," *Les Temps Modernes,* April–May, 1974, cited in Frédéric Martel, *Le rose et le noir: les homosexuels en France depuis 1968* (Paris: Seuil, 1996), 46.
8. Françoise d'Eaubonne, "Le FHAR, origines et illustrations," *La Revue h,* no. 2 (Fall 1996): 21.
9. In French, "L'homosexualité, ce douloureux problème."
10. Some sources have spelled his name as "Guinchat" (for example, Michael Sibalis, "Gay Liberation Comes to France: The Front Homosexuel d'Action Révolutionnaire (FHAR)," *French History and Civilization. Papers from the George Rudé Seminar,* no. 1, 2005) while others such as Eaubonne have remembered it as "Guinchard."
11. Eaubonne, "Le FHAR, origines et illustrations," 21 (In fact, the actual words were "Don't talk to us any more about your suffering" according to the transcript of the show as reprinted in *La Revue h,* no. 1 [Summer 1996]: 59).
12. Eaubonne, "Le FHAR, origines et illustrations," 21.
13. Ibid.
14. Girard, *Le mouvement homosexuel,* 82.
15. The name under which the FHAR registered at the prefecture, however, was the *"Front humanitaire anti-raciste,"* evidence perhaps that in the earliest days of the FHAR, a fear of censure lingered (Girard, *Le mouvement homosexuel,* 82).

16. Marie-Jo Bonnet, "Gay Mimesis and Misogyny: Two Aspects of the Same Refusal of the Other?" *Journal of Homosexuality* 41, no. 3/4 (2001), 268.
17. Bonnet, "Gay Mimesis," 268.
18. Daniel Guérin quoted in Laurent Muhleisen, "Daniel Guérin, militant de l'émancipation homosexuelle," September 2004, http://raforum.info/article.php3?id_article=1841 (accessed January 20, 2007).
19. Bill Marshall, *Guy Hocquenghem* (London: Pluto Press, 1996), 1.
20. Gérard Bach-Ignasse, personal interview by author, Paris, France, May 2, 1997.
21. "Plateforme du Sexpol," supplement to *Antinorm* 3, 11.
22. Ibid.
23. Ibid.
24. Ibid.
25. Ibid.
26. Gay Maës and Anne-Marie Fauret, "Homosexualité et socialisme," *Antinorm*, no. 1 (December 1972–January 1973), 3.
27. See memories of this in Jacques Girard, "Entretien, en mai 1992, de Jacques Girard avec Alain Huet," August 22, 1999, http://www.multimania.com/jgir/huet.htm (accessed 12 June 2004).
28. Girard, "Entretien, en mai 1992," 4.
29. Guy Hocquenghem, *Le désir homosexual* (Paris: Fayard, 2000), 179.
30. Interview with the FHAR, *Actuel*, February 17, 1972, quoted in Girard, *Le mouvement homosexuel*, 94.
31. Girard, *Le mouvement homosexuel*, 84.
32. "Editorial de l'Antinorm," supplement to *Antinorm* 3, 3.
33. "Homosexualité et Politique," *La Canaille* 2 (February 1976), 11.
34. "Principes Fondamentaux de la Charte d'Adhésion au Groupe de Libération Homosexuelle," *Journal du GLH*, no. 0 (June 1976), 1.
35. Ibid.
36. *Anales du GLH 14-XII: Veculs*, no. 1 (Summer 1976).
37. "Principes Fondamentaux," 1.
38. Jan-Paul Pouliquen, personal interview by author, Paris, France, April 3, 1997.
39. Gérard Bach-Ignasse, "Homo comme hétéro," *Sexpol*, no. 8 (May–June 1976), 1.
40. Ibid.
41. "Note 2 Sur la pédérastie," *Anales du GLH 14-XII: Veculs*, no. 1 (Summer 1976): 1.
42. Alain Huet, "Extraits des débats du week-end des 26/27 juin, (suite)," *Anales du GLH 14-XII: Veculs*, no. 1 (Summer 1976).
43. Ibid.
44. Jan-Paul Pouliquen, personal interview by author, Paris, France, April 3, 1997.
45. Girard, *Le mouvement homosexuel*, 176.
46. Janine Mossuz-Lavau, *Les Lois de l'amour: les politiques de la sexualité de 1950 à nos jours* (Paris: Payot, 1991), 270.

47. Janine Mossuz-Lavau, *Les Lois de l'amour: les politiques de la sexualité de 1950 à nos jours* (Paris: Payot, 1991), 270.
48. Gérard Bach-Igansse, "Questions pour le mouvement homosexuel," *Parti Pris*, November 15–December 15, 1980.
49. Michael Sibalis, "Gay Liberation Comes to France: The Front Homosexuel d'Action Révolutionnaire (FHAR)," *French History and Civilization. Papers from the George Rudé Seminar*, no. 1 (2005), 275.
50. *Journal officiel*, Sénat, no. 261, Projet de loi, February 8, 1978.
51. When the senate's first bill arrived on the floor of the national assembly on April 11, 1980, the Deputies, led by Jean Foyer of the rightist RPR. party, voted to keep only the part concerned with the repeal of the 1960 law and to eliminate the part of the bill having to do with the repeal of 1942 law. The bill was thus sent back to the senate for a second reading, but the senators voted to put the part on the repeal of 1942 law back in the bill, before sending it back to the national assembly. On June 24, 1980, the national assembly decided to eliminate once again the section related to the repeal of 1942 law, and sent the bill back to the senate for a third reading. This time, the senate, under Senator Etienne Dailly's guidance – the senator who would turn out to be most hostile to the repeal of the 1942 law – decided to end its defense of the repeal of 1942 law, and sent a bill to the national assembly that dealt only with the repeal of the 1960 law. Upon receiving this from the senate, the Assembly adopted the bill on November 19, 1980 during its third reading.
52. *Journal officiel*, Sénat, no. 43, May 23, 1980, 2086
53. *Journal officiel*, Sénat, no. 43, May 23, 1980, 2098.
54. For example, out of 269 children treated for sexual molestation at the Children's Hospital in Denver, Colorado, between July 1, 1991 and June 30, 1992, 237 (or 88%) were molested by adults who referred to themselves as heterosexual, 30 (or 11%) by adults for whom the sexual orientation was not determined, and 2 (or 0.8%) by adults who referred to themselves as homosexual. (Carole Jenny, Thomas A. Roesler, and Kimberly L. Poyer "Are Children at Risk for Sexual Abuse by Homosexuals?" *Pediatrics* 94 [1994], 41–4).
55. Conseil Constitutionnel, Decision no. 80–125 D.C., December 19, 1980 [emphasis added].
56. "A propos d'un procès," *Le Monde*, January 26, 1977, 24.
57. Jacqueline Rémy, "Libération sexuelle: Le devoir d'inventaire," *L'Express*, March 1, 2001, 82. Michel Foucault discussed the petition in "Sexuality Morality and the Law," trans. Alan Sheridan, in *Michel Foucault: Politics, Philosophy, Culture: Interviews and Other Writings*. ed. Lawrence D. Kritzman (New York: Routledge, 1988), 271–85.
58. Law of August 4, 1982, no. 82–683, *Journal officiel "Lois et Décrets,"* August 5, 1982, 2502. In fact, the final passage of the law had been preceded by a series of back and forth exchanges between the national assembly and the senate. More specifically, the legislative process went as follows: On November 6, 1981, a bill (Proposition 527) to repeal the 1942 law was submitted to the national assembly by the Socialist Deputy, Raymond Forni.

Members in the national assembly energetically debated the bill, with some Socialists believing that if the bill were adopted in its original form, the senate would have blocked its passage until the very end. Eventually, the bill was adopted by the Assembly on December 20, 1981; but was rejected by senate on May 5, 1982. On June 24, 1982, the Assembly began a second reading of the bill and adopted it for a second time. Once again it was rejected by the senate on July 8, 1982. Eventually, a co-partisan committee was formed, but it was unable to reach agreement on a text acceptable to both assemblies. In its third reading, the Assembly adopted the original text on July 21, 1982; the senate rejected it on July 23, 1982; the Assembly voted on it definitively in its fourth reading on July 27, 1982 (Mossuz-Lavau, *Les Lois de l'amour*, 272–3).

59. Dailly became the spokesperson in the senate for those who defended the existence of Paragraph 2 of Article 331. In his speeches before the senate, it is clear the Dailly felt a good amount of disgust for homosexuality: "To suppress the crime of the second paragraph of Article 331 of the Penal Code under these conditions would be reprehensible, and this suppression whether you want it or not, would certainly be interpreted and would be in any case exploited as an encouragement or at least the recognition of the fact that homosexuality is from this point on accepted as a normal sexual practice.... Go ahead and ask all the fathers and mothers in this country! Go ahead and ask them if they believe it is appropriate for us to legalize homosexual acts involving their children between 15 and 18! Also, ask them if they are not specifically counting on the Senate to put up an obstacle to such a legalization!" ("Rapport de M. Etienne Dailly," *Journal officiel*, Sénat, no. 314, Annex to the oral testimony from the session of May 4, 1982, 9–10)

60. "Rapport de M. Etienne Dailly," 10.

61. Ibid.

62. Ibid.

63. *Journal officiel*, Sénat, Débats Parlemenatires – C.R. Discussion from the second reading, Second session of June 24, 1982, 3852.

64. J.J. Eff, "Il a 15 ans, il est libre!" *Gai pied,* September 1982, 9.

65. In French: "L'homosexualité sera bourgeoise ou elle ne passera pas." Bach-Ignasse, "Homo comme hétéro."

# 3   French Homosexuals Build a more Stately Closet

1. Portions of this chapter appear in Scott Gunther, "Building a More Stately Closet: French Gay Movements since the Early 1980s," *Journal of the History of Sexuality* 13, no. 3 (2004): 326–47. They are reprinted here with the journal's permission. The choice of the poem that introduces this chapter was inspired by a presentation by Donald Doub, of San Francisco State University, entitled "Building More Stately Closets," given on October 11, 1998, at "Queer Theories: a National Conference on Gay and Lesbian Studies," held at the University of Nevada, Reno.

2. From Oliver Wendell Holmes, "The Chambered Nautilus," in *Familiar Quotations*, ed. John Bartlett, 10th ed. (Boston: Little, Brown, and Company, 1919), quotation 6939.

3. The notable exception in this timeline is the *Comité d'urgence anti-répression homosexuelle* (CUARH). However, it is not as exceptional as this chart might indicate, since while it is true that the CUARH did not dissolve entirely between 1979 and 1981, it did lose most of its membership and underwent a restructuring of its goals so as to bring it more in line with the prevailing political ideas of the early 1980s. Therefore, while the association survived technically intact, it would be misleading to see this as a simple continuation of its earlier, 1970s self.

4. *Webster's New World Dictionary*, Second College Ed. (Cleveland, OH, 1986), 716.

5. It is important to note that this process of exclusion occurred primarily at the level of representations made by lesbians and gays of themselves. The intent is to avoid suggesting that in the 1980s, lesbians and gays were collectively repressing some innate desire for pedophilia, pederasty, promiscuity, sadomasochism, transvestitism, or public sex, but rather, that at the level of representations, those who had no interest in these practices began to present themselves under the new label of "gay" and to distance themselves from the minority which did have an interest in these practices. In representations of homosexuality in the 1970s, the homosexuals who did have an interest in these practices were put together with those who did not – it was a time when little distinction was made between acceptable and unacceptable homosexuality. In the 1980s, however, the distinction between acceptable and unacceptable became increasingly visible. This is quite different from saying that in the '80s, within every lesbian or gay person there was a pedophile, a pederast, a sadomasochist, a transsexual, a transvestite, or a practitioner of public sex waiting to get out.

6. Steven Green, *Foucault's Panopticon*, January 1999, *The Theory Site*, July 25, 1999, http://www.leeds.ac.uk/ics/ctr-fou3.htm.

7. "Ghetto" is a term used by some French gay political actors to describe what in the American context might simply be referred to as a "community." According to Jacques Girard, the first political group to use the expression "gay ghetto" was the early 1970s *Front homosexuel d'action révolutionnaire* (Girard, "Entretien, en mai 1992").

8. Jean Le Bitoux, "Marcher dans le gai Marais," *La revue h*, no. 1, July 16, 1997, http://www.france.qrd.org/media/revue-h/001/marcher. html (accessed June 12, 2004).

9. Michael Sibalis, "Urban Space and Homosexuality: The Example of the Marais, Paris' 'Gay Ghetto'," *Urban Studies*, 41, no. 9 (2004), 1745.

10. Ibid.

11. Michaël Pollak, "L'homosexualité masculine, ou le bonheur dans le ghetto?" *Sexualités occidentales*, eds. Philippe Ariès and André Béjin (Paris: Seuil, 1982), 56.

12. There is some reason to doubt that the early Gay Pride parades were actually signs of normalization. The first parades were small and were dominated

by the presence of transvestites and those who came to watch them. By the end of the 1980s, however, the parade's participants grew significantly in number as the parade shifted its attention away from transvestites, toward the broader group of socially acceptable homosexuals.

13. "Souvenez-vous, mili-tantes," *Programme Gay Pride Paris 1994*, L'Association gay pride, June 1994, 13.

14. Le Bitoux, "Marcher dans le gai Marais."

15. Foucault, Michel, "The Eye of Power," *Power/Knowledge* (New York: Pantheon Books, 1981).

16. Frédéric Martel, *La longue marche des gays* (Paris: Gallimard, 2002), 59.

17. "*Arcadie* ou la préhistoire du mouvement gai," *Masques: Revue des homosexualités* 15 (1982), 85.

18. Y.E., "La fin d'*Arcadie*?", 7.

19. Ibid.

20. *Le Gai pied*, no. 1 (February 1979), 1.

21. Jean Le Bitoux, "Le guêpier des années *Gai pied*," Gais et Lesbiennes Branchés, September 2002, http://www.france.qrd.org/media/gai%20pied/ (accessed December 19, 2006).

22. Letter from Gérard Vappereau. Directeur de publication, *Gai pied hebdo*, September 10, 1992, 7.

23. Denis Provencher, *Queer French: Globalization, Language, and Sexual Citizenship in France* (Aldershot: Ashgate, 2007), 14.

24. Jean Le Bitoux, "Le guêpier des années *Gai pied*."

25. G.B., "Une loi peut en cacher une autre," *Gai pied hebdo*, July 6–12, 1985, 5.

26. Martel, *La longue Marche des gays*, 59.

27. Martel, *La longue Marche des gays*, 60.

28. Joseph-Marie Hulewicz, "Réflexion: La phobie de l'homosexualité," *Gai pied hebdo*, October 29, 1992, 13.

29. Jan-Paul Pouliquen, personal interview by author, Paris, France, April 3, 1997.

30. "La politique, ça vous fait bander?: aujourd'hui, le 'militante-isme' c'est pas très câblé!" *Gai pied hebdo*, June 30–July 5, 1985, 22–4.

31. "La politique, ça vous fait bander," 24.

32. Marco Lemaire, "Gais pour la liberté, un nouveau carburant," *Gai pied hebdo*, 26 January 26–February 1, 1985, 8.

33. Frédéric Martel, *The Pink and the Black: Homosexuals in France Since 1968* (Stanford: Stanford University Press, 1999), 214.

34. David Caron, *AIDS in French Culture: Social Ills, Literary Cures* (Madison: University of Wisconsin Press, 2001), 155.

35. Caron, *AIDS in French Culture*, 154.

36. Caron, *AIDS in French Culture*, 154–5.

37. Ibid.

38. In English, "The new CUARH has arrived!" The statement alludes to the announcements made each November for the wine, *Beaujolais nouveau*, which appear in café windows all over France: "Le Beaujolais Nouveau est arrivé!"

39. Claude Cocand, "Le CUARH nouveau est arrivé," *Gai pied hebdo,* October 12–18, 1985, 12.
40. Lemaire, "Gais pour la liberté," 24.
41. Law of July 25, 1985, no. 85–772, *Journal officiel "Lois et Décrets,"* July 26, 1985, 8471.
42. See for example, X.L., "Le rendez-vous gai de SOS Racisme," *Gai pied hebdo,* October 19–25, 1985, 5.
43. "Manifeste du GPL," *Gai pied hebdo,* December 22, 1984–January 4, 1985, 3.
44. Francis Lacombe, "Tous à la marche," *Gai pied hebdo,* June 22–28, 1985, 6.
45. In French, "touche pas à mes mœurs" and "touche pas à mon pote."
46. P. Roy, "SOS Racisme à la Concorde le 15 juin," *Gai pied hebdo,* June 8–14, 1985, 6.
47. Malek Boutih, "Contributions," in *Pour le PaCS,* ed. Michel Taube (Paris: L'écart, 1999), 71–2.
48. X.L., "Le rendez-vous gai," 5.
49. *Journal officiel.* Assemblée Nationale. First Session. May 23, 1985: 1104. Not everyone viewed the association of sexism with homophobia positively. During the legislative debates, Deputy Louis Boyer explained his opposition: "Besides the fact that the term [lifestyle] is excessively vague, it would encourage an association between women and homosexuals, which would be entirely negative for the feminine gender" (Hervé Liffran, "L'Assemblée nationale dit oui aux homos," *Gai pied hebdo,* July 6–12, 1985, 5).
50. *Journal officiel,* Sénat, no. 279, Projet de loi, May 13, 1981.
51. Some articles have falsely credited Jean-Pierre Michel, rather than Robert Badinter, with developing the term "based on lifestyle" (see, for example, N.B., "Touche pas à mes moeurs," *Gai pied hebdo,* June 1–7, 1985, 6).
52. Jean-Pierre Michel, personal interview by author, Paris, France, April 3, 1997. Former president of the CUARH, Jan-Paul Pouliquen, offered a similar explanation: "We, at the CUARH had proposed the term 'sexual orientation'. But there were some risks with that: for one, the term 'sexual orientation' could refer to pedophilia. It's true that lifestyle could also refer to pedophilia, but no one would imagine that. Besides, we saw the case of the guy who got fired for long hair, and well, having long hair, that's covered by 'lifestyle'" (Pouliquen interview).
53. *Journal officiel.* Assemblée Nationale, Débats parlementaires, First Session, May 23, 1985.
54. In the discussion that follows, the term "PaCS" refers to all the various forms of legally recognized same-sex partnerships proposed during the 1990s. The proposed structure went under a variety of acronyms including, the PaCS, the CUC, and the CUS. The term used in the final draft was "PaCS."
55. Gérard Bach-Ignasse, personal interview by author, Paris, France, May 2, 1997.
56. Pouliquen interview.
57. Michel interview.

58. Ibid.

59. Pouliquen interview.

60. Clarisse Fabre and Eric Fassin, *Liberté, égalité, sexualités* (Paris: Belfond/Le Monde, 2003), 50.

61. Arrêt n° 652, February 24, 2006, Cour de cassation – Première chambre civile, http://www.courdecassation.fr/article577.html (accessed June 16, 2007)

62. Another justification was based on psychoanalytical arguments dealing with the need for a "symbolic order that respects sexual difference." These kinds of arguments were presented in the legislative debates, particularly by Irène Théry, author of a report titled "Couple filiation et parenté aujourd'hui." (Fiammetta Venner and Joël Métreau, "Le PaCS, Enfin!" *Têtu,* November 1999, 61).

63. The slogan in French: "Un enfant, un papa et une maman; un enfant, deux papas, bonjour les dégâts!" is modeled after a public service advertisement in France against drunk driving, which said "Deux verres, ça va; trois verres, bonjour les dégâts!"

64. Bach-Ignasse interview.

65. Fassin, Eric and Michel Feher. "Parité et PaCS: anatomie politique d'un rapport." In *Au-delà du PaCS: l'expertise familiale à l'épreuve de l'homosexualité,* edited by Daniel Borillo, Eric Fassin, and Marcela Lacub. (Paris: Presses Universitaires de France, 1999), 24–5.

66. Fabre and Fassin, *Liberté, égalité, sexualités,* 28.

67. The only evidence of deportations of French homosexuals comes from the region of Alsace, a region which was at the time a part of Germany. In that region, the numbers were probably not as high as those that Pouliquen mentions here, although there are of course many difficulties associated with establishing a precise number. See, for example, Pierre Seel, *I, Pierre Seel, Deported Homosexual: A Memoir of Nazi Terror* (New York: Basic Books, 1995).

68. Pouliquen interview.

69. Observatoire du PacS, http://www.chez.com/obspacs/ (accessed April 13, 2004).

70. Michel interview.

71. Fiammetta Venner and Joël Métreau, "Le PaCS, Enfin!" *Têtu,* 39, November 1999, 54.

72. Venner and Métreau, "Le PaCS, Enfin!", 54.

73. Law number 2004–1486 of December 30, 2004.

74. Julien Picquart, *Pour en finir avec l'homophobie* (Paris: Editions Léo Scheer, 2005), 135.

75. Constant Rémond, "Projet de loi contre l'homophobie : halte à la dérive liberticide!" *Conscience Politique,* June 29, 2004, http://www.conscience-politique.org/2004/remondloicontrehomophobie.htm (accessed March 20, 2007).

76. Laurent Joffrin, "Une loi liberticide contre les injures," *Le nouvel observateur,* December 16, 2004, 66.

77. Picquart, *Pour en finir avec l'homophobie,* 135.

## 4   "Outing" the French Gay Media (The 1990s and 2000s)

1. Portions of this chapter appear in Scott Gunther, "Not 'communautaire' but 'identitaire': Linguistic Acrobatics on France's PinkTV," *Contemporary French Civilization* 31, no. 2 (2007). They are reprinted here with the journal's permission.
2. Jumana Farouky, "Absolutely Pink," *Time Magazine*, Europe Edition, November 10, 2003, http://www.time.com/time/europe/magazine/article/0,13005,901031110-536184,00.htm (accessed October 17, 2006).
3. *Préférences Mag*, March–April 2004, 3.
4. "Edito," *Têtu*, July–August 1995, 7.
5. The figure of 3 percent comes from a survey of *Têtu*'s readers conducted in 2005. "Etude TNS Sofrès-*Têtu*: Qui sont les homos d'aujourd'hui?" *Têtu*, May 2005, 79.
6. See for example, Marieke de Mooij, *Global Marketing and Advertising: Understanding Cultural Paradoxes*, 2nd edition (New York: Sage, 2005).
7. "Edito," *Gai pied*, May 1979, 2.
8. Transcript of online chat from April 25, 2005, with Thomas Doustaly, editor in chief of *Têtu*, http://www.tetu.com/rubrique/mag/mag_dialogue1.php (accessed October 31, 2006).
9. "Courrier des lecteurs," *Têtu*, September 1995, 67.
10. Ibid.
11. Ibid.
12. Ibid.
13. Ibid.
14. "Courrier des lecteurs," *Têtu*, October 1995, 79.
15. "Courrier des lecteurs," *Têtu*, July–August 1996, 100.
16. Ibid.
17. In addition to these tensions, *Têtu* has faced the challenge of of developing a discursive style that blends elements of Americanized, globalized gay culture with a French twist in order for it to work for French gays. In his analysis of this "cooperative discourse" in *Têtu*, Denis Provencher explains that "Such discourse may include specific references to gay people and events in France. These include references to France's long literary tradition and French writers on homosexuality such as Marcel Proust, Colette, André Gide, and Jean Genet, as well as more contemporary events such as Gay Pride Paris, the prohibition against gay-pride rainbow flags in Le Marais (Paris neighborhood frequented largely by gays and lesbians), the 1999 discussion about the civil union bill (PaCS), as well as the role of French political figures who support equal rights for all French citizens. ... Also in the 'French' tradition, *Têtu* journalists embarked on a gay 'Tour de France' by both interviewing and featuring everyday gays and lesbians from such French regions as Languedoc, Alsace, Bretagne and Normandie." (Denis Provencher, *Queer French*, 45).
18. Didier Lestrade, "*Têtu*: une histoire," *Têtu*, May 2005, 92–6.

19. The data for Figure 4.1 come from a sampling of 6 issues of *Têtu* maga-zine made up of the September issues for 1995, 1997, 1999, 2001, 2003, and 2005. I developed 52 categories for articles and 49 categories for advertising. For each issue, I calculated the number of 1/12ths of a page devoted to each of these categories (I chose 1/12 of a page as the basic unit, because almost all the pages' contents fit neatly into spaces meas-uring 1/12, 1/6, 1/3, 1/4 or 1/2 of page, all of which could be easily con-verted to 1/12ths). Of the 52 categories, 23 were associated with "hard news" and 29 with "soft news."

20. "Etude TNS Sofrès-*Têtu*," 80.

21. "Etude TNS Sofrès-*Têtu*," 81.

22. Transcript of online chat from April 25, 2005, with Thomas Doustaly, editor in chief of *Têtu*, http://www.tetu.com/rubrique/mag/mag_dialogue1.php (accessed October 31, 2006).

23. The data for Tables 4.1, 4.2, and 4.3 come from an analysis of 30 issues of *Têtu* magazine, including the magazine's first 10 issues in 1995 and 1996, along with the February and September issues for each year from 1997 to 2006. For each issue, I counted the number of pages devoted to the following categories: (1) articles written specifically for gay male read-ers, (2) articles written specifically for lesbian readers, (3) articles that deliberately included information for both gay male and lesbian readers, (4) articles whose intended readers' gender and sexual identities were undeterminable, neutral, or irrelevant, (5) advertising specifically target-ing gay male readers, (6) advertising specifically targeting lesbian read-ers, (7) advertising deliberately and explicitly targeting both gay male and lesbian readers, and (8) advertising whose intended targets' gender and sexual identities were undeterminable or irrelevant. Since virtually all of *Têtu*'s readers identify themselves as homosexual, if an article or advertisement was made specifically for men (whether heterosexual or homosexual), I counted it as an article or advertisement for gay male readers; likewise, if an article or advertisement was made specifically for women (whether heterosexual or homosexual), I counted it as an article or advertisement for lesbian readers. I computed averages for each year and then averaged the values for these 12 years to get an overall average. Finally, to determine the space devoted to gay men's articles, I added the values from category (1) and half of the value of category (3). Similarly, to determine the space devoted to articles for lesbians, I added the values from category (2) and half of the value of those in category (3).

24. The sociologist, Marie-Hélène Bourcier, was recently involved in a law suit brought by *Têtu* against her for defamation. The magazine was suing her because she had said in an interview with the Swiss gay magazine *360°* that she had heard from an anonymous informant that women were excluded from editorial meetings at *Têtu*. The court eventually found in Bourcier's favor.

25. Didier Lestrade, "'*Têtu*': une histoire," *Têtu*, May 2005, 95–6.

26. "Courrier des lecteurs," *Têtu*, September 2000, 98.

27. "Courrier des lecteurs," *Têtu*, February 2005, 13.
28. Ibid.
29. Peggy Deweppe, "Edito," *La dixième muse*, May 2003, 4.
30. "Etude TNS Sofrès-*Têtu*," 82.
31. Frédéric Praï, "Premières abonnées, premiers abonnés," *Têtu*, May 2005, 88.
32. *Préférences Mag*, March–April 2004, 3.
33. In the anniversary issue, Bertrand Millet retells a story told to him by an anonymous witness of how the magazine came about. He said that the title was decided in September 2003 (Bertrand Millet, "C'est arrivé l'an dernier," *Préf*, March–April 2005, 20).
34. http://www.genremagazine.com/corp/about.cfm (accessed January 4, 2007).
35. *Préférences Mag*, March–April 2004, 3.
36. *Préférences Mag*, May–June 2004, 3.
37. *Préférences Mag*, March–April 2004, 126.
38. Lionel Chassing, "Qu'est-ce qu'on a tant pour être heureux," *Préférences Mag*, March–April 2004, 108–9.
39. Gonzague de Larcoque, "De la norme faisons table rase," *Préférences Mag*, July–August 2004, 102.
40. *Préf*, November–December 2005, cover.
41. *Préf*, May–June 2006, cover.
42. *Préf*, July–August 2006, cover.
43. "Courrier des lecteurs," *Préf*, November–December 2006, 16.
44. "Courrier des lecteurs," *Préférences Mag*, September–October 2004, 8.
45. Doreen Carvajal, "France's Pink TV: A Rosy Outlook?" *The International Herald Tribune*, November 8, 2004, 11.
46. "Pink TV, La liberté, ça se regarde!" http://www.PinkTV.fr/indexf.php?fls=1 (accessed January 5, 2006) [emphasis added].
47. Carvajal, "France's Pink TV," 11.
48. One might ask why PinkTV, whose self-image is so resistant to American definitions of identity, has chosen to use an English word for its own name. Of course, "pink" is not the only English word in the French gay and lesbian vernacular, which also includes expressions like "le coming out," "le backroom," and "le queer." Could it be that the use of English words allows French gays and lesbians to distance themselves from the hypocrisy involved in maintaining a universalist discourse while indulging in various elements of a communautaire lifestyle? Perhaps one can believe that as long as the concepts do not actually enter the French language, French society has managed to avoid being contaminated by these alien concepts?
49. Fabre and Fassin, *Liberté, égalité, sexualités*, 26
50. Provencher, *Queer French*, 18.
51. Guy Dutheil, "Pink TV ne veut pas se limiter aux seuls homosexuels," *Le Monde*, September 30, 2004.
52. Ixchel Delaporte, "Une Télévision En Rose," *L'Humanité*, September 30, 2004.

53. *Trésor de la langue française en 16 volumes*, 1981, 5, 1136.
54. *Dictionnaire de l'Académie françiase, en deux volumes* (Paris: Editions Julliard, 1994) I, 962.
55. *Le Robert: dictionnaire de la langue française, en neuf volumes* (Paris: Dictionnaire Le Robert, 1989).
56. http://forum.wordreference.com/showthread.php?t=7439> (accessed January 27, 2006).
57. http://forum.wordreference.com/showthread.php?t=69492 (accessed January 27, 2006).
58. http://forum.wordreference.com/showthread.php?t=7439 (accessed January 27, 2006).
59. http://forum.wordreference.com/showthread.php?t=69492 (accessed January 27, 2006).
60. The word "identitaire" could not be found for example in the 9-volume *Le Robert: dictionnaire de la langue française* (1989), the 2-volume *Dictionnaire de l'Académie Français* (1994), the 6-volume *Emile Littré: Dictionnaire de la langue française* (2004), the 7-volume *Grand Larousse de la langue française* (1989), and the 16-volume *Trésor de la langue française* (1981).
61. *Le Grand Robert, en 6 volumes* (Paris: Dictionnaires Le Robert, 2001) III, 2037. The dictionary adds that the word only exists as a technical or scholarly term and is not used in ordinary spoken French.
62. Wikipedia contributors, "Communautarisme identitaire," Wikipédia, http://fr.wikipedia.org/w/index.php?title=Communautarisme_ identitaire&oldid=13189448 (accessed January 4, 2007).
63. Elizabeth Bryant, "Gay Channel Debuts in France," *United Press International*, October 25, 2004.
64. "Pink TV débarque sur les petits écrans," *Le Nouvel observateur*, October 23, 2004, http://archquo.nouvelobs.com/cgi/articles?ad=culture/20041023. OBS9814.html&host=http://permanent.nouvelobs.com/ (accessed February 2, 2006).
65. Caroline Comte, *PinkTV, Dossier de Presse*, September 28, 2004, 9.
66. Pascal Houzelot, "Edito," *PinkTV, Dossier de Presse*, September 28, 2004, 3.
67. "Pink TV : Dix visages pour une télé pas sage," *Têtu*, October 2004, 41.
68. "Nulle Part Ailleurs," *E-llico*, http://v2.e-llico.com/article-retro.htm? articleID=115&rubrique=tele&oldRubrique=tele (accessed December 6, 2006).
69. "Nulle Part Ailleurs."
70. Catherine Nardone, "Interview: Marie Labory & Christophe Beaugrand," *Toute la télé*, August 16, 2005, http://www.toutelatele.com/article.php3?id_ article=4730&var_recherche=Marie+Labory+ (accessed November 20, 2006).
71. Nardone, "Interview."
72. Carvajal, "France's Pink TV," 11.
73. "About Logo," *Logo Online*, http://www.logoonline.com/about/ (accessed January 6, 2006).

74. The data for Figures 4.3, 4.4, 4.5, and 4.6 come from an analysis of 91 days of PinkTV programming, including every 8th day of programming from January 4, 2005 to December 25, 2006. The period of 8 days was selected to ensure a cycling through the days of the week. For each day, the number of minutes dedicated to each program was recorded. Programs were first put into the following categories: (1) entertainment, (2) news, documentaries, and debate shows, (3) high culture, which included operas, classical music concerts, theater, and reports on literature and art, (4) nonpornographic films, and (5) pornographic films. Programs were also identified as (1) for the GLBT community in general, (2) for lesbians specifically, (3) programs whose intended viewers' gender and sexual identities were undeterminable or irrelevant, (4) for gay men specifically, (5) programs dealing with gay icons, drag queens, gay camp, or kitsch.

75. *PinkTV, Saison 2 (2005–2006) Dossier de Presse*, September 22, 2005, 4.

76. *PinkTV, Fiche de presentation*, http://www.tf1pub.fr/supports/presentation/42.php, (accessed January 4, 2007).

77. Julien Bellver and Benoît Daragon, "Pascal Houzelot : Je suis fier d'user de ma position pour faire avancer la cause gay," Le Mag', March 20, 2006, http://www.imedias.biz/lemag/lemag-pascal-houzelot-je-suis-fier-duser-de-ma-position-pour-fai-320.php (accessed December 13, 2006).

78. Louis Maury, "PinkTV a un an: interview avec Pierre Garnier," *Têtu*, November 2005, 45.

79. Le Set Episode 111, Paris: PinkTV, April 5, 2006.

80. Le Set Episode 113, April 10, 2006.

81. Le Set Episode 115, April 12, 2006.

82. Nardone, "Interview."

83. Ibid.

84. In French, "vieille gouine revêche." Louis Maury, "En clair, 'Le Set' fait peau neuve," *Têtu*, September 2005, 82.

85. Le Set Episode 111, April 5, 2006.

86. Le Set Episode 115, April 12, 2006.

87. Ibid.

88. Le Set Episode 118, April 25, 2006.

89. This is based on a quantitative analysis of all the guests invited on Le Set between January 1, 2006 and June 1, 2006. The running average for this 5-month period varied only slightly between 39 percent and 42 percent for the number of female guests.

90. This is based on a qualitative study of every episode of Le Set for the month of April 2006. Over the course of the month, 86 percent of the female guests were heterosexual, 14 percent were lesbian, and 0 percent were unidentifiable. For male guests, 41 percent were heterosexual, 35 percent were homosexual, 11 percent were unidentifiable, and 6 percent were bisexual.

91. This is based on a qualitative study of every episode of Le Set for the month of April 2006.

92. Le Set Episode 118, April 25, 2006.

93. Le Set Episode 119, April 26, 2006.

94. Le Set Episode 114, April 11, 2006.
95. Le Set Episode 117, April 24, 2006.
96. *PinkTV, Saison 3 (2006–2007) Dossier de Presse*, October 2006, 3 [emphasis added].
97. Alex Taylor, "Le Coming Out?" Le Débat, Paris: PinkTV, September 25, 2006.

## Conclusion: Queer, *Made in France*

1. Portions of this section appear in Scott Gunther, "Alors, Are We 'Queer' Yet?" *The Gay & Lesbian Review* 12, no. 3 (2005), 23–5. They are reprinted here with the journal's permission.
2. *Lawrence and Garner v. Texas*, 539 US 558 (2003).
3. Joshua Gamson, "Must Identity Movements Self-Destruct?" *Social Perspectives in Lesbian and Gay Studies* (New York: Routledge, 1998), 593.
4. Frédéric Martel, *The Pink and the Black*, 355.
5. Catherine Deschamps, "Intro-mission," in *Q comme Queer* (Lille: Gai Kitsch Camp, 1998), 11.
6. Marie-Hélène Bourcier, "Le 'nous' du zoo," in *Q comme Queer*, 94.
7. Bourcier, "Le 'nous' du zoo," 96.
8. Marie Klonaris and Katerina Thomadaki, "Filmer les identities sexuelles comme une complexité en mouvement," in *Queer: repenser les identités* (Paris: Presses Universitaires de France, 2003), 84.
9. Klonaris and Thomadaki, "Filmer les identities sexuelles," 87.
10. Klonaris and Thomadaki, "Filmer les identities sexuelles," 84.
11. Beatriz Preciado, "Il faut queeriser l'université," in *Queer: repenser les identités*, 81.
12. Provencher, *Queer French*, 193.
13. William J. Poulin-Deltour, "French Gay Activism and the American Referent in Contemporary France," *The French Review* 78, no. 1 (2004), 118.
14. Poulin-Deltour, "French Gay Activism," 125.
15. Bruce LaBruce, "La France: un je ne sais quoi déjà queer," in *Queer: repenser les identités*, 108.

# Bibliography

## Books and articles

Albert, Nicole. *Saphisme et décadence dans Paris fin-de-siècle*. Paris: La Martinière, 2005.

Aldrich, Robert. "Homosexuality in the French Colonies." *Journal of Homosexuality* 41, no. 3/4 (2001): 201–18.

"Arcadie ou la préhistoire du mouvement gai." *Masques: Revue des homosexualités*, no. 15 (1982): 85.

Ariès, Philippe and André Béjin, eds. *Sexualités Occidentales. Communications* 35. Paris: Point Seuil, 1982.

Bachelot, Roselyne. *Le Pacs entre haine et amour*. Paris: Plon, 1999.

Bach-Ignasse, Gérard. "Homo comme hétéro." *Sexpol*, May–June 1976.

———. *Homosexualité: La Reconnaissance?* Boulogne-Bilancourt: Espace Nuit, 1988.

———. "Questions pour le mouvement homosexuel." *Parti pris*, November 15–December 15, 1980.

Barbadette, Gilles and Michel Carassou. *Paris Gay 1925*. Paris: Presses de Renaissance, 1981.

Benstock, Shari. "Paris lesbianism and the politics of reaction, 1900–1940." In *Hidden from History*, edited by Martin Bauml Duberman, Martha Vicinus, and George Chauncey. New York: Penguin, 1989.

Blanc, Olivier. "The 'Italian Taste' in the Time of Louis XVI, 1774–92." *Journal of Homosexuality* 41, no. 3/4 (2001): 69–84.

Boisson, Jean. *Le Triangle Rose. La déportation des homosexuels (1933–1945)*. Paris: Robert Laffont, 1988.

Boninchi, Marc. *Vichy et l'ordre moral*. Paris: Presses Universitaires de France, 2005.

Bonnet, Marie-Jo. *Un choix sans équivoque*. Paris: Denoel, 1981.

———. "Gay Mimesis and Misogyny: Two Aspects of the Same Refusal of the Other?" *Journal of Homosexuality* 41, no. 3/4 (2001): 265–80.

———. *Les relations amoureuses entre les femmes du XVIe au XXe siècle*. Paris: Odile Jacob, 1995.

Borrillo, Daniel. *Homosexualités et droit*. Paris: Presses Universitaires de France, 1999.

———. *Que sais-je: L'Homophobie*. Paris: Presses Universitaires de France, 2001.

———. "Statut juridique de l'homosexualité et droits de l'homme." *Cahiers Gai Kitsch Camp: Un sujet inclassable? Approches sociologiques, littéraires et juridiques des homosexualités* (February 1995): 100.

Borrillo, Daniel, Eric Fassin, and Marcela Lacub. *Au-delà du PaCS*. Paris: Presses Universitaires de France, 2001.

Borrillo, Daniel and Jack Lang. *Homosexuels. Quels droits?* Paris: Dalloz-Sirey, 2007.

Borrillo, Daniel and Pierre Lascoumes. *Le Pacs, les homosexuels et la gauche.* Paris: La Découverte, 2002.

Bory, Jean-Louis and Guy Hocquenghem. *Comment nous appelez-vous déja?* Paris: Calmann-Lévy, 1977.

Bourcier, Marie-Hélène. "Le 'nous' du zoo." In *Q comme Queer.* Lille: Gai Kitsch Camp, 1998.

———. *Queer Zones.* Paris: Balland, 2006.

Boutih, Malek. "Contributions." In *Pour le PaCS,* edited by Michel Taube. Paris: L'Ecart, 1999.

Brassaï *The Secret Paris of the 30's.* New York: Pantheon, 1981.

Brassart, Alain. *L'homosexualité dans le cinéma français.* Paris: Nouveau Monde, 2007.

Buisson-Fenet, Hélène. *Un sexe problématique: L'Église et l'homosexualité masculine en France (1971–2000).* Saint-Denis: Presse Universitaire de Vincennes, 2004.

Canler, Louis. *Mémoires de Canler: ancien chef du service de sûreté.* Brussels: 1862. Reprint, Paris: Mercure de France, 2006.

Carlier, Félix. *Les Deux prostitutions.* Paris: 1887 (reprinted, Paris: Le Sycomore, 1981).

Caron, David. *AIDS in French Culture: Social Ills, Literary Cures.* Madison: University of Wisconsin Press, 2001.

Casselaer, Catherine van. *Lot's wife: Lesbian Paris, 1890–1914.* Liverpool: Janus, 1986.

Casta-Rosaz, Fabienne. *Histoire de la sexualité en Occident.* Paris: La Martinière, 2004.

Choquette, Leslie. "Homosexuals in the City: Representations of Lesbian and Gay Space in Nineteenth-Century Paris." *Journal of Homosexuality* 41, no. 3/4 (2001): 149–68.

Conseil Constitutionnel. Decision no. 80–125 D.C. December 19, 1980.

Copley, Antony. *Sexual Moralities in France, 1790–1980: New ideas on the family, divorce, and homosexuality.* New York: Routledge, 1989.

Corraze, Jacques. *Que sais-je: l'homosexualité.* 8th edition. Paris: Presses Universitaires de France, 2006.

Courouve, Claude. "1791 Law Reform in France." *Gay Books Bulletin* 12 (1985): 9–10.

———. "L'Amour socratique du *Dictionnaire philosophique* de Voltaire." *Cahiers Gai Kitsch Camp* 24 (1994): 79–87.

———. *Les Assemblées de la manchette: documents sur l'amour masculin au XVIIIe siècle.* Paris: Courouve, 1987.

———. "Sodomy trials in France." *Gay Books Bulletin* 1 (1978): 22–3, 26.

———. *Vocabulaire de l'homosexualité masculine.* Paris: Payot, 1985.

Cusset, François. *Queer critics: La littérature française déshabillée par ses homo-lecteurs.* Paris: Presses Universitaires de France, 2002.

Danet, Jean. "Discours juridique et perversions sexuelles (XIXe et XXe siècles)." *Famille et Politique* 6 (1977).

Daniel, Marc. "A propos de Cambacérès." *Revue Arcadie* no. 95 (1961): 553–68.

Daniel, Marc. "Histoire de la législation pénale française concernant l'homosexualité I." *Revue Arcadie* no. 96 (1961): 618–27.

——. "Histoire de la législation pénale française concernant l'homosexualité II." *Revue Arcadie* no. 97 (1962): 10–29.

Daniel, Marc and André Baudry. *Les Homosexuels*. Tournai: Casterman, 1973.

Dean, Carolyn J. *The Frail Social Body: Pornography, Homosexuality, and Other Fantasies in Interwar France*. Berkeley: University of California Press, 2000.

Delmar, Michaël. *Petit lexique illustré du gay-savoir*. Paris: Scali, 2007.

Derai, Yves. *Le gay pouvoir: Enquête sur la République bleu blanc rose*. Paris: Ramsay, 2003.

Deschamps, Catherine. "Intro-mission." In *Q comme Queer*. Lille: Gai Kitsch Camp, 1998.

Devoucoux du Buisson, François. *Les Khmers rose. Essai sur l'idéologie homosexuelle*. Paris: Blanche, 2003.

Dobelbower, Nicholas. "*Les Chevaliers de la guirlande*: Cellmates in Restoration France." *Journal of Homosexuality* 41, no. 3/4 (2001): 131–48.

Eaubonne, Françoise d'. "Le FHAR, origines et illustrations." *La Revue h* 2 (1996): 21.

Erber, Nancy. "The French Trials of Oscar Wilde." *Journal of the History of Sexuality* 6, no. 4 (1996): 549–88.

——. "Queer Follies: Effeminacy and Aestheticism in fin-de-siècle France, the Case of Baron d'Adelsward Fersen and Count de Warren." In *Disorder in the Court: Trials and Sexual Conflict at the Turn of the Century*, edited by George Robb and Nancy Erber. New York: New York University Press, 1999.

Eribon, Didier. *Dictionnaire des cultures gays et lesbiennes*. Paris: Larousse, 2003.

——. *Réflexions sur la question gay*. Paris: Fayard, 1999.

——. *Sur cet instant fragile*. Paris: Fayard, 2004.

Estrée, Paul d'. *Les infâmes sous l'ancien régime: documents historiques recueillis à la Bibliothèque Nationale et à l'Arsénal (dépôt des papiers de la Bastille)*. Lille: Gai Kitsch Camp, 1994.

"Etude TNS Sofrès-*Têtu*: Qui sont les homos d'aujourd'hui?" *Têtu*, May 2005, 79–80.

Ewald, François and Pierre Antoine Fenet, eds. *Naissance du Code civil*. Paris: Flammarion, 1989.

Fabre, Clarisse and Eric Fassin. *Liberté, égalité, sexualités*. Paris: Belfond/Le Monde, 2003.

Fassin, Eric. "Homosexualité et marriage aux Etats-Unis: Histoire d'une polémique." *Actes de la recherche en sciences sociales*, no. 125 (1998): 63.

——. *L'inversion de la question homosexuelle*. Paris: Amsterdam, 2005.

Fassin, Eric and Michel Feher. "Parité et PaCS: anatomie politique d'un rapport." In *Au-delà du PaCS: l'expertise familiale à l'épreuve de l'homosexualité*, edited by Daniel Borillo, Eric Fassin, and Marcela Lacub. Paris: Presses Universitaires de France, 1999.

Florand, Jean-Marc and Karim Achoui. *Homosexuels quels sont vos droits?* Paris: Librairie Générale de Droit et de Jurisprudence, 1993.

Foucault, Michel. "Sexuality Morality and the Law." Translated by Alan Sheridan. In *Michel Foucault: Politics, Philosophy, Culture: Interviews and Other Writings*, edited by Lawrence D. Kritzman. New York: Routledge, 1988.

Gamson, Joshua. "Must Identity Movements Self-Destruct?" In *Social Perspectives in Lesbian and Gay Studies*, edited by Peter M. Nardi and Beth E. Schneider. New York: Routledge, 1998.

Garcia, Daniel. *La Folle histoire du marriage gay.* Paris: Flammarion, 2004.

Garnier, Paul. "Rapport médico-légal." *Annales d'hygiène publique et de médecine mentale.* Tome XXXIII. 3rd Series. January–June 1895.

Girard, Jacques. "Entretien, en mai 1992, de Jacques Girard avec Alain Huet." August 22, 1999, http://www.multimania.com/jgir/huet.htm.

———. *Le mouvement homosexuel en France 1945–1980.* Paris: Syros, 1981.

Gross, Martine, Stéphane Guillemarre, Lilian Mathie, and Caroline Mécary. *Homosexualité, mariage et filiation: Pour en finir avec les discriminations.* Paris: Syllepse, 2005.

Guérin, Daniel. "La Répression de l'homosexualité en France." *Shakespeare et Gide en correctionnelle?* Paris: Editions du Scorpion, 1959. 93–121.

Gunther, Scott. "*Alors*, Are We 'Queer' Yet?" *The Gay & Lesbian Review* 12, no. 3 (2005): 23–5.

———. "Building a More Stately Closet: French Gay Movements since the Early 1980s." *Journal of the History of Sexuality* 13, no. 3 (2004): 326–47.

———. "Le Marais: The Indifferent Ghetto." *Harvard Gay and Lesbian Review* 6, no. 1 (1999): 34, 36.

———. "Not '*communautaire*' but '*identitaire*': Linguistic Acrobatics on France's PinkTV." *Contemporary French Civilization* 31, no. 2 (2007).

Gury, Christian. *L'homosexuel et la loi.* Paris: Aire, 1981.

Hahn, Pierre. *Nos ancêtres les pervers: la vie des homosexuels sous le Second Empire.* Paris: Olivier Orban, 1979.

Heathcote, Owen, Alex Hughes, and James S. Williams, eds. *Gay Signatures: Gay and Lesbian Theory, Fiction and Film in France, 1945–1995.* London: Palgrave Macmillan, 1998.

Higgs, David, ed. *Queer Sites: Gay Urban Histories since 1600.* New York: Routledge, 1999.

Hinds, Leonard. "Female Friendship as the Foundation of Love in Madeleine de Scudéry's 'Histoire de Sapho'." *Journal of Homosexuality* 41, no. 3/4 (2001): 23–36.

Hocquenghem, Guy. *Le désir homosexual.* Paris: Fayard, 2000.

"Homosexualité et Politique." *La Canaille,* February 1976, 11.

"Des Homosexuels sous condition." *Gai pied,* May 1982, 12.

Houzelot, Pascal. "Edito." *PinkTV Dossier de Presse.* Paris: PinkTV, September 28, 2004: 3.

Huas, Jeanine. *L'homosexualité au temps de Proust.* Dinard: Danclau, 1992.

Huet, Alain. "Extraits des débats du week-end des 26/27 juin, (suite)." *Anales du GLH 14-XII,* Summer 1976.

"Interview with the FHAR." *Actuel,* February 17, 1972.

Jablonski, Olivier. "The Birth of a French Homosexual Press in the 1950s." *Journal of Homosexuality* 41, no. 3/4 (2001): 233–48.

Jackson, Julian. "Sex, Politics and Morality in France, 1954–1982." *History Workshop Journal* 61 (2006): 77–102.

Joffrin, Laurent. "Une loi liberticide contre les injures." *Le nouvel observateur,* December 16, 2004, 66.

*Journal officiel.* Assemblée Nationale. no. 19. annex no. 733. Projet de loi. July 6, 1960.

——. Assemblée Nationale. no. 26. annex no. 819. Projet de loi. July 21, 1960.

——. Assemblée Nationale. no. 51. July 19, 1960: 1981.

——. Assemblée Nationale. Débats Parlemenatires. First Session. May 23, 1985: 1103–4.

——. Sénat. no. 43. May 23, 1980.

——. Sénat. no. 261. Projet de loi. February 8, 1978.

——. Sénat. no. 279. Projet de loi. May 13, 1981.

——. Sénat. Débats Parlemenatires – C.R. Discussion from the second reading. Second session of June 24, 1982: 3852.

*Jurisclasseur.* Correctional Tribunal of the Seine. February 9, 1965.

*Jurisclasseur Pénal.* Articles 330–333. "Attentat aux Moeurs." 21.

Klonaris, Marie and Katerina Thomadaki. "Filmer les identities sexuelles comme une complexité en mouvement." In *Queer: repenser les identités (Rue Descartes, no. 40).* Paris: Presses Universitaires de France, 2003.

Knibiehler, Yvonne. *La sexualité et l'histoire.* Paris: Odile Jacob, 2002.

LaBruce, Bruce. "La France: un je ne sais quoi déjà queer." In *Queer: repenser les identités (Rue Descartes, no. 40).* Paris: Presses Universitaires de France, 2003.

Lamou, Yves. "Le Point sur le délit d'outrages publics à la pudeur." *Revue Arcadie* (1975): 350–3.

Larivière, Michel. *Les amours masculines.* Paris: Lieu Commun, 2006.

Le Bitoux, Jean. *Citoyen de seconde zone.* Paris: Hachette, 2003.

——. "The Construction of a Political and Media Presence: The Homosexual Liberation Groups in France between 1975 and 1978." *Journal of Homosexuality* 41, no. 3/4 (2001): 249–64.

——. "Le guêpier des années *Gai pied.*" Gais et Lesbiennes Branchés. September 2002, http://www.france.qrd.org/media/gai%20pied/.

——. "Marcher dans le gai Marais." *La revue h* 1 (1997).

Leroy-Forgeot, Flora. *Les Enfants du Pacs: Réalités de l'homoparentalité.* Paris: Presses Universitaires de France, 2000.

——. *Histoire juridique de l'homosexualité en Europe.* Paris: Presses Universitaires de France, 1997.

Lesselier, Claudie. *Aspects de l'expérience lesbienne en France, 1930–1968.* Mémoire de D.E.A. de sociologie. Université de Paris-VIII, under the direction of R. Castel, November 1987.

Lestrade, Didier. *ACT UP: Une histoire.* Paris: Denoël, 2000.

——. "*Têtu*: une histoire." *Têtu,* May 2005, 92–6.

Lever, Maurice. *Les bûchers de Sodome.* Paris: Favard, 1985.

Maës, Gay and Anne-Marie Fauret. "Homosexualité et socialisme." *Antinorm* 1 (December 1972–January 1973): 3.

Marshall, Bill. *Guy Hocquenghem.* London: Pluto Press, 1996.

Martel, Frédéric. *La longue marche des gays.* Paris: Gallimard, 2002.

——. *Matériaux pour servir à l'histoire des homosexuels en France: chronologie, bibliographie, 1968–1996.* Lille: Gai Kitsch Camp, 1996.

——. *Le rose et le noir: les homosexuels en France depuis 1968.* Paris: Seuil, 1996. Translated by Jane Marie Todd under the title *The Pink and the Black: Homosexuals in France since 1968* (Stanford: Stanford University Press, 1999).

Maugue, Annelise. *L'Identité masculine en crise au tournant du siècle, 1871–1914.* Paris: Rivages, 2006.

McCaffrey, Enda. *The Gay Republic: Sexuality, Citizenship and Subversion in France.* London: Ashgate, 2005.

Mécary, Caroline and Géraud de la Pradelle. *Que sais-je: Les droits des homosexuel/les.* 3rd edition. Paris: Presses Universitaires de France, 2003.

Mécary, Caroline and Flora Leroy-Forgeot. *Que sais-je: Le Pacs.* Paris: Presses Universitaires de France, 2001.

Medès-Leite, Rommel. *Les Bisexualités: une notion en quête de sens.* Paris: Calmann-Lèvy, 1996.

——. "Un sujet inclassable? Approches sociologiques, littéraires et juridiques des homosexualités." *Cahiers Gai Kitsch Camp* no. 28 (1995).

——. "'Brutal Passion' and 'Depraved Taste': The Case of Jacques-François Pascal." *Journal of Homosexuality* 41, no. 3/4 (2001): 85–104.

——. "Commissioner Foucault , Inspector Noël, and the 'Pederasts' of Paris, 1780–83." *Journal of Social History* 32 (1998): 287–307.

——. "'Nocturnal Birds' in the Champs-Elysées: Police and Pederasty in Pre-Revolutionary Paris." *GLQ: A Journal of Lesbian and Gay Studies* 8 (2002): 425–32.

——. "Sodomites and Police in Paris, 1715." *Journal of Homosexuality* 42, no. 3 (2002): 103–28.

Merrick, Jeffrey and Bryant T. Ragan, Jr., eds. *Homosexuality in Early Modern France: A Documentary Collection.* New York: Oxford University Press, 2001.

——, eds. *Homosexuality in Modern France.* New York: Oxford University Press, 1996.

Merrick, Jeffrey and Michael Sibalis, eds. *Homosexuality in French History and Culture.* New York: Harrington Park Press, 2001.

Merriman, John. *Police Stories: Building the French State, 1815–1851.* Oxford: Oxford University Press, 2005.

Mossuz-Lavau, Janine. *Les lois de l'amour: les politiques de la sexualité de 1950 à nos jours.* Paris: Payot, 1991.

Murat, Laure. *La loi du genre: Une histoire culturelle du troisième sexe.* Paris: Fayard, 2006.

Nye, Robert A. *Masculinity and Male Codes of Honor in Modern France.* Oxford: Oxford University Press, 1993.

Passay, Jean-Jacques. "L'incapacité juridique au plaisir." *Recherches* 37 (1979).

Peniston, William. "Love and Death in Gay Paris: Homosexuality and Criminality in the 1870s." In *Homosexuality in Modern France*, edited by Jeffrey Merrick and Bryant T. Ragan, Jr. New York: Oxford University Press, 1996.

———. *Pederasts and Others: Urban Culture and Sexual Identity in Nineteenth-Century Paris*. New York: Harrington Park Press, 2004.

———. "Pederasts, Prostitutes, and Pickpockets in Paris of the 1870s." *Journal of Homosexuality* 41, no. 3/4 (2001): 169–88.

———. "A Public Offense against Decency: the Trial of the Count de Germiny and the 'Moral Order' of the Third Republic." In *Disorder in the Court: Trials and Sexual Conflict at the Turn of the Century*, edited by George Robb and Nancy Erber. New York: New York University Press, 1999.

Peniston, William and Nancy Erber, eds. *Queer Lives: Men's Autobiographies from 19th-Century France*. Lincoln: University of Nebraska Press, 2007.

*PinkTV Saison 1 (2004–2005) Dossier de Presse*. Paris: PinkTV. September 2004.

*PinkTV Saison 2 (2005–2006) Dossier de Presse*. Paris: PinkTV. September 2005.

*PinkTV Saison 3 (2006–2007) Dossier de Presse*. Paris: PinkTV. October 2006.

"Plateforme du Sexpol." supplement to *Antinorm* 3: 11.

Picquart, Julien. *Pour en finir avec l'homophobie*. Paris: Editions Léo Scheer, 2005.

Pollak, Michaël. "L'homosexualité masculine, ou le bonheur dans le ghetto?" In *Sexualités occidentales*, edited by Philippe Ariès and André Béjin. Paris: Seuil, 1982.

Poulin-Deltour, William J. "French Gay Activism and the American Referent in Contemporary France." *The French Review* 78, no. 1 (2004): 118–27.

Pouliquen, Jan-Paul. *Contrat d'union civile: le dossier*. Paris: Humoeurs, 1994.

Preciado, Beatriz. "Il faut *queer*iser l'université." In *Queer: repenser les identités (Rue Descartes, no. 40)*. Paris: Presses Universitaires de France, 2003.

"Principes Fondamentaux de la Charte d'Adhésion au Groupe de Libération Homosexuelle." *Journal du GLH* 0, June 1976.

"Prolétaires de tous les pays, caressez-vous!" *Gulliver* 1, November 1972.

Proth, Bruno. *Lieux de drague: Scènes et coulisses d'une sexualité masculine*. Paris: Octares, 2002.

Provencher, Denis. *Queer French: Globalization, Language, and Sexual Citizenship in France*. Aldershot: Ashgate, 2007.

———. "Queer Studies in France." *Contemporary French Civilization* 27, no. 2 (2003): 406–16.

Ragan, Bryant T., Jr. "The Enlightenment Confronts Homosexuality." In *Homosexuality in Modern France*, edited by Jeffrey Merrick and Bryant T. Ragan, Jr. New York: Oxford University Press, 1996.

Rambach, Anne and Marine Rambach. *La Culture gaie et lesbienne*. Paris: Fayard, 2003.

"Rapport de M. Etienne Dailly." *Journal officiel*. Senate. no. 314. Annex to the oral testimony from the session of May 4, 1982.

Rassat, Michèle-Laure. "Inceste et Droit Pénal." *La Semaine Juridique* I.2614 (1974).

Rémond, Constant. "Projet de loi contre l'homophobie: halte à la dérive liberticide!" *Conscience Politique*, June 29, 2004. http://www.conscience-politique.org/2004/remondloicontrehomophobie.htm.

Rémy, Jacqueline. "Libération sexuelle: Le devoir d'inventaire." *L'Express*, March 1, 2001, 82.

Revenin, Régis. *Homosexualité et prostitution masculines à Paris: 1870–1918.* Paris: L'Harmattan, 2005.

Rey, Michel. "Paris Homosexuals Create a Lifestyle, 1700–1750." *Eighteenth-Century Life 9*, no. 3 (1985): 179–91.

——. "Police and Sodomy in 18th Century Paris: From Sin to Disorder." *Journal of Homosexuality* 16, nos. 1, 2 (1988).

Robb, George and Nancy Erber, eds. *Disorder in the Court: Trials and Sexual Conflict at the Turn of the Century.* New York: New York University Press, 1999.

Robb, Graham. *Strangers: Homosexual Love in the Nineteenth Century.* London: Picador, 2003.

Robinson, David Michael. "The Abominable Madame de Murat." *Journal of Homosexuality* 41, no. 3/4 (2001): 53–68.

Rosario, Vernon A., II. *The Erotic Imagination: French Histories of Perversity.* New York: Oxford University Press, 1997

——. "Phantastical Pollutions: The Public Threat of Private Vice in France." In *Solitary Pleasures: The Historical, Literary, and Artistic Discourses of Autoeroticism*, edited by Paula Bennett and Vernon Rosario II, 101–30. New York: Routledge, 1995.

——. "Pointy Penises, Fashion Crimes, and Hysterical Mollies: The Pederasts' Inversions." In *Homosexuality in Modern France*, edited by Jeffrey Merrick and Bryant T. Ragan, Jr. New York: Oxford University Press, 1996.

Roussel, Yves. "Le mouvement homosexuel français face aux stratégies identitaires." *Les Temps Modernes* May–June 1995.

Rubenstein, William B., ed. *Lesbians, Gay Men, and the Law.* New York: The New Press, 1993.

Schachter, Marc D. " 'That Friendship Which Possesses the Soul': Montaigne Loves La Boétie." *Journal of Homosexuality* 41, no. 3/4 (2001): 5–22.

Schehr, Lawrence R. *Alcibiades at the Door: Gay Discourses in French Literature.* Stanford: Stanford University Press, 1995.

——. *French Gay Modernism.* Champaign: University of Illinois Press, 2004.

——. *The Shock of Men: Homosexual Hermeneutics in French Writing.* Stanford: Stanford University Press, 1995.

Schlick, Jean and Marie Zimmermann. *L'Homosexuel(le) dans les sociétés civiles et religieuses.* Strasbourg: Cerdic, 1985.

Schultz, Gretchen. "La Rage du plaisir et la rage de la douleur: Lesbian Pleasure and Suffering in Fin-de-siècle French Literature and Sexology." In *Pleasure and Pain*, edited by David Evans and Kate Griffiths. Amsterdam: Rodopi, 2009.

Seel, Pierre. *I, Pierre Seel, Deported Homosexual: A Memoir of Nazi Terror*. New York: Basic Books, 1995. Originally published as *Moi, Pierre Seel, déporté homosexuel*. Paris: Calmann-Lévy, 1994.

Seifert, Lewis C. "Masculinity and Satires of 'Sodomites' in France, 1660–1715." *Journal of Homosexuality* 41, no. 3/4 (2001): 37–52.

Sibalis, Michael D. "Gay Liberation Comes to France: The Front Homosexuel d'Action Révolutionnaire (FHAR)." *French History and Civilization. Papers from the George Rudé Seminar* 1 (2005): 265–76.

——. "Homophobia, Vichy France, and the 'Crime of Homosexuality': The Origins of the Ordinance of 6 August 1942." *GLQ: A Journal of Lesbian and Gay Studies* 8, no. 3 (2002): 301–18.

——. "Jean-Jacques-Régis Cambacérès." In *Who's Who in Contemporary Gay & Lesbian History: From Antiquity to World War II*, edited by Robert Aldrich and Garry Wotherspoon. London: Routledge, 2001.

——. "The Palais-Royal and the Homosexual Subculture of Nineteenth-Century Paris." *Journal of Homosexuality* 41, no. 3/4 (2001): 117–30.

——. "Paul Mirguet." In *Who's Who in Contemporary Gay & Lesbian History: From Antiquity to World War II*, edited by Robert Aldrich and Garry Wotherspoon. London: Routledge, 2001.

——. "The Regulation of Male Homosexuality in Revolutionary and Napoleonic France, 1789–1815." In *Homosexuality in Modern France*, edited by Jeffrey Merrick and Bryant T. Ragan, Jr. New York: Oxford University Press, 1996.

——. "Urban Space and Homosexuality: The Example of the Marais, Paris' 'Gay Ghetto'." *Urban Studies* 41, no. 9 (2004): 1739–58.

Sidéris, Georges. "*Folles*, Swells, Effeminates, and Homophiles in Saint-Germain -des-Prés of the 1950s: A New 'Precious" Society?'" *Journal of Homosexuality* 41, no. 3/4 (2001): 219–32.

Stambolian, George and Elaine Marks. *Homosexualities and French Literature*. Ithaca: Cornell University Press, 1990.

Stychin, Carl F. "Civil Solidarity or Fragmented Identities? The Politics of Sexuality and Citizenship in France." *Social & Legal Studies* 10, no. 3 (2001): 347–75.

Surkis, Judith. *Sexing the Citizen: Morality and Masculinity in France, 1870–1920*. Ithaca: Cornell University Press, 2006.

Tamagne, Florence. *Histoire de l'homosexualité en Europe: Berlin, Londres, Paris 1919–1939*. Paris: Seuil, 2000.

Tardieu, Ambroise. *Etude sur les attentats aux moeurs*. 6th edition. Paris: Baillère, 1873.

Taube, Michel, ed. *Pour le PaCS*. Paris: L'écart, 1999.

Thompson, Victoria. "Creating Boundaries: Homosexuality and the Changing Social Order in France, 1830–1870." In *Homosexuality in Modern France*, edited by Jeffrey Merrick and Bryant T. Ragan, Jr. New York: Oxford University Press, 1996.

Tin, Louis-Georges. *Dictionnaire de l'homophobie*. Paris: Presses Universitaires de France, 2003.

——, ed. *Homosexualités: expression/repression*. Paris: Stock, 2000.

Tissot, Olivier de. *La liberté sexuelle et la loi*. Paris: Balland, 1984.

Van der Meer, Theo. "Sodomy and the Pursuit of a Third Sex in the Early Modern Period." In *Third Sex/Third Gender: Beyond Sexual Dimorphism in Culture and History*, edited by Gilbert Herdt. New York: Zone Books, 1994.

Verdrager, Pierre. *L'Homosexualité dans tous ses états*. Paris: Empêcheurs de Penser en Rond, 2007.

Weiss, Andrea. *Paris was a Woman: Portraits from the Left Bank*. New York: HarperCollins, 1996.

Wilson, Michael L. *"Drames d'amour des pédérastes*: Male Same-Sex Sexuality in Belle Epoque Print Culture." *Journal of Homosexuality* 41, no. 3/4 (2001): 189–200.

Wolfgang, Aurora. "A passion between women: The case of Germaine de Staël and Juliette Récamier." *Women in French Studies* 7 (1999): 66–78.

## Interviews

Anonymous interviews with members of the Paris-based association *Les gais retraités*, February–May 1995, Paris, France.

Gérard Bach-Ignasse, personal interview by author, Paris, France, May 2, 1997.

Jan-Paul Pouliquen, personal interview by author, Paris, France, April 3, 1997.

Jean-Pierre Michel, personal interview by author, Paris, France, April 3, 1997.

### Archival materials
### Archives de la Préfecture de Police de Paris, 1 bis rue des Carmes

"Pédérastes, 1820–1882" (A.P.P. DA 230 (6)), 428 pieces, 1st division, 2nd bureau, Document number 318.

"Pédérastes, 1820–1882" (A.P.P. DA 230 (6)), 428 pieces, 1st division, 2nd bureau, Document number 325.

"Pédérastes, 1820–1882" (A.P.P. DA 230 (6)), 428 pieces, 1st division, 2nd bureau, Document number 328.

"Pédérastes, 1820–1882" (A.P.P. DA 230 (6)), 428 pieces, 1st division, 2nd bureau, Document number 411.

"Pédérastes, 1820–1882" (A.P.P. DA 230 (6)), 428 pieces, 1st division, 2nd bureau, Document number 413.

"Pédérastes, 1820–1882" (A.P.P. DA 230 (6)), 428 pieces, 1st division, 2nd bureau, Document number 423.

### Archives of *Gai pied*, rue Keller, Paris

Dossiers de Presse "Gai pied"
"Pédéraste" Binders, numbers 1–14, January 1965–February 1977.

### Centre des archives contemporaines, Fontainebleau

AN, CAC, 950395, article 4 (D. 2718), dossier 60-SL: Attentats à la pudeur (1945), January 9, 1934 letter from Minister of the Navy.

AN, CAC, 950395, article 4 (D. 2718), dossier 60-SL: Attentats à la pudeur (1945), January 27, 1934 letter from Minister of Justice.

AN, CAC, 950395, article 4 (D. 2718), dossier 60-SL: Attentats à la pudeur (1945), May 9, 1939 letter from the members of the jury in the Roger Neuville trial.

AN, CAC, 950395, article 4 (D. 2718), dossier 60-SL: Attentats à la pudeur (1945), June 10, 1939 report from Médan.

AN, CAC, 950395, article 4 (D. 2718), dossier 60-SL: Attentats à la pudeur (1945), December 22, 1941 report from the deputy public prosecutor of Toulon.

AN, CAC, 950395, article 4 (D. 2718), dossier 60-SL: Attentats à la pudeur (1945), March 13, 1942 note for the Minister of Justice.

AN, CAC, 950395, article 4 (D. 2718), dossier 60-SL: Attentats à la pudeur (1945), April 14, 1942 letter from Admiral Darlan.

AN, CAC, 950395, article 4 (D. 2718), dossier 60-SL: Attentats à la pudeur (1945), November 9, 1942 letter from Admiral Auphan

## Laws

Law of July 19–22, 1791. Chapter II, Article 8 (established crime of public indecency).

Law of September 25–October 6, 1791 (ratified the 1791 Penal Code, which left out the crime of sodomy ).

Law of 13 March 1863 (raised the age of sexual majority for everyone from 11 to 13).

Law of August 6, 1942 (modified Article 334 of the Penal Code by setting the age of sexual majority for homosexuals at 21 – the age for heterosexuals remained 13). Published in *Journal officiel "Lois et Décrets"* August 27, 1942: 2922.

Ordinance of February 8, 1945, no. 45–190 (moved the 1942 law from Article 334 to Article 331 of the Penal Code; kept age for homosexuals at 21 and raised the age for heterosexuals to 15). Published in *Journal officiel "Lois et Décrets"* February 9, 1945: 650.

Ordinance of July 30, 1960, no. 60–773 (the "Mirguet" amendment, which granted the government the power to take "all measures needed to fight against homosexuality"). Published in *Journal officiel "Lois et Décrets"* August 2, 1960: 7130.

Ordinance of November 25, 1960, no. 60–1245 (the government's response to the Mirguet amendment, which modified Article 330 of the Penal Code and increased the penalty for public indecency for homosexuals). Published in *Journal officiel "Lois et Décrets"* November 27, 1960: 10603.

Law of July 5, 1974, no. 74–631, article 15 (lowered age of civil majority for everyone to 18, which inadvertently had the effect of lowering the age of sexual majority for homosexuals to 18). Published in *Journal officiel "Lois et Décrets"* July 7, 1974: 7099.

Law of December 23, 1980, no. 80–1041 (repealed the "Mirguet" amendment of 1960). Published in *Journal officiel "Lois et Décrets"* December 24, 1980: 3028.

Law of August 4, 1982, no. 82–683 (repealed the "Vichy" law from 1942). Published in *Journal officiel "Lois et Décrets"* August 5, 1982: 2502.

Law of July 25, 1985, no. 85–772 (the anti-discrimination law). Published in *Journal officiel "Lois et Décrets"* July 26, 1985: 8471.

Law of November 15, 1999, no. 99–944 (the PaCS law). Published in *Journal officiel "Lois et Décrets"* November 16, 1999: 16959.

Law of December 30, 2004, no. 2004–1486 (the anti-homophobia law).

# Index